Online Teaching Beginner's Guide

Your Step-by-Step Roadmap on How to Set Up Secure Zoom Classes, Organize Interactive Google Classroom Spaces, and Keep Students Engaged From Day One

I0081422

Frank Nelson

TABLE OF CONTENTS

Book 1 - Zoom for Beginners

Introduction

What is Zoom and Why It's Important for Online Teaching

In the age of digital transformation, the way we approach teaching has changed dramatically. Zoom, a video conferencing platform originally designed for virtual meetings, has become a cornerstone of online education. Whether you're teaching a classroom of students, conducting one-on-one tutoring, or hosting webinars for professional development, Zoom provides educators with the ability to connect with students in real time, regardless of geographical location.

Zoom offers features that make it ideal for online teaching, such as screen sharing, video conferencing, recording options, and real-time interactions. As the global demand for online education grows, Zoom has emerged as one of the most popular platforms for educators at all levels. Its versatility, ease of use, and scalability make it an essential tool for teachers, enabling them to create a dynamic learning environment even when students are miles apart. Understanding how to use Zoom effectively is crucial for anyone looking to succeed in virtual teaching, whether you're just starting or you've been teaching online for years.

The Evolution of Virtual Learning

The concept of virtual learning isn't new, but it has grown significantly in the past two decades. The advent of the internet, coupled with innovations in technology, made online education a feasible option for students around the world. Initially, virtual learning was limited to pre-recorded lessons and email exchanges, but as the internet matured, so did the capabilities for live, interactive education.

Zoom's emergence in the mid-2010s revolutionized virtual learning by providing a user-friendly platform for face-to-face interaction, making it possible for educators to connect with students in real-time, replicate classroom settings, and engage in collaborative learning experiences. The rise of online degree programs, remote work, and the necessity brought on by the COVID-19 pandemic accelerated the adoption of platforms like Zoom in the educational sector.

Today, virtual learning is not only a necessity in emergencies but has become an integral part of the education landscape. Students and educators now expect flexibility and accessibility in their learning environments, and Zoom has positioned itself as a key player in making this transition smooth and effective.

How Zoom Enhances the Online Teaching Experience

Zoom's unique features cater to the needs of online educators, enhancing the teaching experience in ways that traditional classrooms cannot replicate. Here are a few key ways in which Zoom transforms online education:

1. **Real-Time Interaction**: Unlike pre-recorded videos, Zoom allows educators to engage with students in real time, answering questions, facilitating discussions, and guiding activities instantly. This creates a more interactive and personal learning experience.

2. **Breakout Rooms**: Zoom's breakout rooms enable small group discussions or collaborative activities, mimicking the experience of working in small groups in a physical classroom. Teachers can move between rooms to offer support or listen to group discussions, fostering deeper engagement among students.

3. **Screen Sharing and Whiteboard Features**: Teachers can share their screens to present slides, documents, websites, and videos, providing students with a more dynamic and visual learning experience. The whiteboard tool allows teachers to draw or write in real time, facilitating explanations and brainstorming sessions.

4. **Recording and Accessibility**: Zoom allows meetings to be recorded, making it easy for students to revisit lessons and review content. This feature is especially beneficial for students who may need additional time to understand material or those in different time zones.

5. **Polling and Reactions**: Zoom enables teachers to create polls, quizzes, and surveys during class, providing instant feedback on student understanding. Reactions like thumbs up, applause, or laughter allow students to participate in a non-verbal way, making them feel more engaged and involved.

6. **Integration with Learning Management Systems (LMS)**: Zoom seamlessly integrates with many Learning Management Systems, allowing for smooth coordination between classes, grades, and materials. This integration saves time and reduces the need to manage multiple platforms simultaneously.

With all these features, Zoom not only mimics the traditional classroom experience but enhances it by offering tools that promote flexibility, creativity, and collaboration. For educators, mastering Zoom can make the difference between a successful virtual classroom and a disconnected, ineffective one.

Who Should Use This Guide: A Quick Overview for Beginners

This guide is designed for anyone who is new to using Zoom for teaching purposes. Whether you're an educator transitioning from a traditional classroom to an online environment, a tutor seeking a platform for virtual lessons, or someone looking to host online workshops or webinars, this guide will provide you with the knowledge and skills you need to get started with Zoom and enhance your teaching experience.

Who Will Benefit from This Guide?

- **Teachers and Educators**: If you're transitioning to teaching online or looking to improve your virtual teaching skills, this guide will help you master the basics of Zoom, engage students effectively, and implement best practices.

- **Tutors**: Whether you're offering one-on-one lessons or small group sessions, Zoom offers a flexible and interactive space for personalized tutoring. This guide will show you how to maximize Zoom's features to meet the unique needs of your students.

- **Corporate Trainers and Speakers**: If you're conducting webinars, professional development seminars, or training sessions, this guide will help you make the most of Zoom's capabilities for a seamless and engaging experience.

- **Anyone New to Online Teaching**: If you've never used Zoom or online teaching tools before, this guide is for you. We'll start with the basics and walk you through everything you need to know to host effective online classes.

By the end of this guide, you'll feel confident in your ability to set up, run, and engage with your students using Zoom. You'll be equipped with the tools to create an engaging virtual classroom, troubleshoot common issues, and take your online teaching to the next level.

Chapter 1: Getting Started with Zoom

Before diving into online teaching with Zoom, it's crucial to get familiar with the platform and set it up properly. In this chapter, we'll walk you through the essential first steps: downloading and installing Zoom, creating and configuring your account, understanding the interface, and customizing your settings to ensure the best possible teaching experience.

1. Downloading and Installing Zoom

The first step to using Zoom for online teaching is to download and install the application. You can use Zoom on a variety of devices, including your computer, tablet, or smartphone. Here's how to get started:

On a Computer (Windows or Mac):

1. Open your web browser and go to the official Zoom website: https://zoom.us/download.

2. Under the "Zoom Client for Meetings" section, click on the **Download** button. This will download the Zoom installer.

3. Once the download is complete, open the installer to begin the installation process.

4. Follow the on-screen instructions to complete the installation. The installer will automatically place the Zoom application on your computer.

5. After installation, open Zoom by double-clicking the Zoom icon that appears on your desktop or in your Applications folder.

On Mobile Devices (iOS or Android):

1. Open the **App Store** (iOS) or **Google Play Store** (Android) on your device.

2. Search for "Zoom Cloud Meetings" and click **Install**.

3. Once the app is installed, open it, and you're ready to start!

Web Browser Version:

Although Zoom offers a desktop and mobile app, you can also use Zoom through a web browser for quick meetings. Simply go to https://zoom.us/join, click on "Join a Meeting," and follow the prompts.

2. Creating and Configuring Your Zoom Account

Once Zoom is installed, you'll need to create a Zoom account if you don't already have one. A Zoom account is necessary to schedule and host meetings. Here's how to create one:

Creating an Account:

1. Open the Zoom app and click on **Sign Up** or go to https://zoom.us/signup from your browser.

2. You'll be asked to enter an email address. You can either use your work email or a personal email. Zoom also offers the option to sign up via Google or Facebook if you prefer.

3. Once you enter your email address, Zoom will send you a confirmation email. Click on the link in the email to activate your account.

4. After confirming your email, you'll be prompted to enter a name and create a password for your Zoom account. Choose a password that is secure and easy to remember.

5. Once your account is created, you'll be directed to the Zoom dashboard, where you can begin managing your meetings, settings, and profile.

Configuring Your Zoom Account:

1. **Personal Information**: Once logged into your account, navigate to the "Profile" section. Here you can add your display name, profile picture, and any other relevant details about your teaching setup.

2. **Time Zone**: Set your correct time zone to ensure that meeting times are shown accurately.

3. **Integrating with Calendars**: You can link your Google Calendar or Outlook calendar to Zoom for easier scheduling and management of meetings.

4. **Email Notifications**: Under the settings tab, you can adjust email preferences to receive meeting reminders and notifications for upcoming classes.

3. Understanding the Zoom Interface

Now that your Zoom account is set up, it's important to familiarize yourself with the interface. Knowing where everything is located and how to navigate the platform will help you feel more confident when hosting meetings.

Main Zoom Dashboard:

- **Home Tab**: The Home tab is where you can quickly join or schedule meetings, view your upcoming meetings, or start an instant meeting.

- **Meetings Tab**: Here you can manage your scheduled meetings, including the ability to edit, delete, or copy meeting invitations.

- **Contacts Tab**: This tab allows you to manage your contacts, add others to your Zoom account, and create groups for easy communication.

- **Settings Tab**: This section contains all your account settings, where you can customize preferences related to video, audio, notifications, security, and more.

When You Enter a Meeting:

Once you enter a meeting, the Zoom interface consists of several main sections:

- **Video Feed**: Your video feed (and any other participants' videos) will be shown in the middle of the screen.

- **Toolbar**: The toolbar at the bottom of the screen is where you can control key features during the meeting:

  o **Mute/Unmute**: Toggle your microphone on or off.

  o **Stop/Start Video**: Turn your video on or off.

  o **Participants**: See who is in the meeting, mute participants, or manage their settings.

  o **Share Screen**: Share your desktop or a specific window with other participants.

  o **Chat**: Open the chat window to send text messages to everyone or privately to specific participants.

  o **Reactions**: Show virtual reactions like thumbs up or applause during a meeting.

Managing Participants:

When you host a meeting, the "Participants" tab will be especially important. From here, you can:

- Mute/unmute participants.

- Enable/disable video.

- Create breakout rooms.

- Remove participants if needed.

4. Customizing Your Settings for the Best Experience

Customizing your Zoom settings is key to creating a productive and comfortable teaching environment. Here are some essential settings to adjust:

Audio Settings:

1. **Microphone**: Select your preferred microphone input (e.g., your built-in microphone, an external mic, or a headset). You can test your mic here to ensure it works properly.

2. **Speaker**: Select your preferred audio output (e.g., your computer speakers, headphones, etc.).

3. **Enable Original Sound**: If you want the highest quality audio, especially when teaching music or other audio-sensitive subjects, turn on the "Enable Original Sound" option in the advanced audio settings.

Video Settings:

1. **Camera**: Choose your preferred camera (your built-in webcam or an external camera).

2. **Virtual Background**: If you want to appear in front of a custom background (such as a classroom or library), enable this feature.

3. **Touch Up My Appearance**: This feature applies a subtle smoothing effect to your appearance during video meetings, helping you look your best.

4. **Enable HD Video**: If your internet connection allows, enable HD video for a clearer image.

Security Settings:

1. **Password Protection**: Ensure your meetings are password-protected to avoid unauthorized access. You can configure this to apply to all meetings by default.

2. **Waiting Room**: Enable the waiting room feature so you can screen participants before allowing them into your meeting. This is helpful for maintaining a secure and controlled classroom environment.

3. **Meeting Lock**: After all your participants have joined, you can lock the meeting to prevent others from entering.

Host Controls:

1. **Mute Participants Upon Entry**: This setting is helpful for large classes to avoid noise disruptions when participants join.

2. **Disable Video Upon Entry**: Set participants' video to be off when they enter the meeting to ensure they don't appear unprepared.

3. **Allow Participants to Share Screen**: You can restrict who can share their screen (only the host or any participant).

Recording Settings:

1. **Record Automatically**: If you want all meetings to be recorded, you can enable this setting so Zoom automatically starts recording when you begin a meeting.

2. **Cloud Recording**: If you have a paid Zoom account, you can choose to store recordings in the cloud, making it easy to share with students later.

By completing these steps and configuring your Zoom settings, you'll be well-equipped to host professional, interactive, and engaging online classes. The next chapter will dive deeper into hosting your first Zoom meeting, ensuring you're ready to make a great first impression!

Chapter 2: Hosting Your First Meeting

Hosting your first Zoom meeting can be an exciting and rewarding experience. In this chapter, we will walk you through the process of scheduling your meeting, understanding all the important settings and options, sending invitations to your students, and finally, starting and joining your meeting with ease.

1. Scheduling a Zoom Meeting

Scheduling a meeting in Zoom allows you to set the date and time for your online class in advance. It's a simple process that ensures both you and your students are prepared. Here's how to do it:

Steps to Schedule a Meeting:

1. **Open Zoom**: Launch the Zoom app on your desktop or open Zoom via your web browser and sign in to your account.

2. **Click on "Schedule a New Meeting":**

   o If you are using the Zoom desktop app, click on the **"Schedule"** button on the home screen.

   o If using the web version, click on the **"Schedule a New Meeting"** option in the top right corner of the dashboard.

3. **Set Meeting Details**:

   o **Topic**: Enter a title for your meeting. For example, "Introduction to Online Teaching" or "Math Class – Week 1."

   o **Description** (optional): Provide a short description of the meeting's purpose or agenda. This will help participants understand what to expect.

- o **When**: Select the date and time for your meeting. If it's a recurring class, you can enable the recurring option, which allows you to set the meeting to occur at regular intervals (e.g., daily, weekly).

- o **Time Zone**: Make sure to select the correct time zone, especially if you have students from different regions.

4. **Meeting Options**:

- o **Passcode**: You can require a passcode for extra security, ensuring only invited participants can join.

- o **Waiting Room**: If you want to screen your students before they enter, enable the waiting room feature. This will allow you to admit participants one by one or all at once when you're ready.

- o **Video**: Choose whether to start the meeting with your video on or off. You can set this option separately for the host and participants.

- o **Audio**: Choose whether to allow participants to connect via computer audio or phone (or both).

- o **Meeting Options**:

  - Enable **"Mute participants upon entry"** to prevent noise disruptions as your students join the meeting.

  - Enable **"Automatically record meeting"** if you want the session to be recorded for later access (available for paid accounts).

5. **Save the Meeting**: After filling in all the necessary details, click on **"Save"** to finalize your meeting schedule. This will generate a unique meeting link.

2. Understanding Meeting Settings and Options

Zoom offers several settings and options that can help you manage your meeting more effectively, especially as a host. Understanding these settings will allow you to customize your meeting and make it run smoothly.

Host Controls:

- **Mute All Participants**: As the host, you can mute all participants when they enter to prevent noise distractions. You can always unmute them individually as needed.

- **Allow Participants to Unmute Themselves**: This setting controls whether participants can unmute themselves or if you need to give them permission. It's useful for controlling the flow of conversation in larger classes.

- **Spotlight Video**: If you want to make sure that your video feed is always the primary one seen by participants, you can spotlight your video. This is particularly useful when you're the main speaker.

- **Allow Participants to Share Screen**: You can restrict who can share their screen. This is particularly helpful to avoid students sharing irrelevant or distracting content during class. You can allow only the host to share their screen or allow all participants to share their screens.

- **Breakout Rooms**: Breakout rooms allow you to split participants into smaller groups for collaborative activities or discussions. You can set the number of rooms and assign participants manually or let Zoom assign them automatically.

- **Whiteboard**: If you plan to use a whiteboard during your meeting (for writing, drawing, or brainstorming), you can enable this feature. Participants can also be given access to annotate on the whiteboard.

- **Recording Settings**: Decide if you want to record the meeting (either locally on your device or to the cloud). You can also choose whether to record audio, video, and screen sharing during the session.

Security Settings:

- **Lock Meeting**: Once all your students have joined, you can lock the meeting to prevent anyone else from entering. This is an essential security feature for closed, private classes.

- **Remove Participants**: If a participant is being disruptive or not following class rules, you have the option to remove them from the meeting permanently.

- **Report a Participant**: In case of any inappropriate behavior, you can report the participant to Zoom for review.

Other Advanced Settings:

- **Enable Live Transcription**: Zoom provides an automatic transcription feature for your meetings, which will generate live captions for your participants. This can be helpful for students who have hearing impairments or prefer reading along.

- **Q&A and Polling**: You can create polls and allow students to ask questions during the meeting. Polling can be an interactive way to assess student understanding in real time.

3. Sending Invitations to Students

After scheduling your Zoom meeting, it's important to send out invitations to your students so they can join the session. Here's how to do that:

Via Zoom (Email Invitation):

1. **After Scheduling**: Once you've scheduled your meeting and clicked **"Save"**, Zoom will display a meeting link and invitation details.

2. **Click "Copy Invitation"**: This button will copy the full meeting details to your clipboard, including the meeting link, passcode (if applicable), and dial-in phone numbers.

3. **Send the Invitation**: Paste the copied invitation into an email or a messaging platform like Slack, Google Classroom, or Microsoft Teams to send to your students. Include any additional instructions (e.g., materials to review before the meeting).

Via Google Calendar or Outlook:

1. **Syncing with Calendar**: If you linked your Google Calendar or Outlook account to Zoom, you can automatically add your Zoom meeting to your calendar.

2. **Invite Students**: Once your meeting is added to your calendar, you can send invitations directly from the calendar event to your students' email addresses. This ensures they have the meeting details, and it will also show up on their calendars.

Sending a Reminder:

To ensure that your students don't forget about the meeting, consider sending a reminder a few hours or a day before the session. You can do this manually by emailing them or using the reminder feature in your calendar app.

4. Joining and Starting a Meeting

Finally, it's time to join or start your meeting. Whether you are the host or a participant, the process is straightforward.

As the Host:

1. **Start the Meeting**:
   - Open the Zoom app or go to the Zoom website and sign in.
   - Navigate to the **"Meetings"** tab and find the meeting you scheduled.
   - Click **"Start"** to launch the meeting.
   - If the meeting is password-protected, you will be prompted to enter the passcode you set earlier.

2. **Host Controls:**

   o Once the meeting starts, you will have access to the host controls in the toolbar, including managing participants, sharing your screen, starting recordings, and more.

As a Participant:

1. **Join via Link**: When the meeting time arrives, click on the meeting link provided in the invitation. Zoom will open automatically or prompt you to download the app if you haven't done so.

2. **Join via Meeting ID**: If you don't have a link, you can join by manually entering the **Meeting ID** and **Passcode** (if applicable) on the Zoom website or app.

3. **Audio and Video Settings**: Before entering, you will be asked to join with your audio and video settings. You can join the meeting with your microphone and camera on or off.

Meeting Etiquette:

- **Introduce Yourself**: As the host, take a moment to introduce yourself and go over the structure of the meeting.

- **Engage Students**: Ask questions, encourage participation, and make use of Zoom's interactive tools (e.g., chat, polls, and reactions).

- **Monitor the Chat**: Keep an eye on the chat for questions or comments from your students. You can address them during or after the session.

By now, you should feel comfortable scheduling, inviting, and running your first Zoom meeting. In the next chapter, we'll explore how to use Zoom's key features to keep your students engaged and make the most of your virtual teaching experience!

Chapter 3: Essential Zoom Features for Teachers

In this chapter, we'll explore the core features of Zoom that are most relevant to teachers. Understanding how to use these features will help you maintain control over your online classroom, keep students engaged, and enhance your teaching experience. From basic controls to advanced tools like breakout rooms and screen sharing, mastering these features will set you up for success in any online teaching setting.

1. The Basics: Mute, Video, and Screen Sharing

Let's start with the fundamental features that you'll use in every meeting: **Mute**, **Video**, and **Screen Sharing**. These are the most essential tools for maintaining a smooth and professional class.

Mute/Unmute:

- **Why It's Important**: As a host, you will likely want to mute participants when they enter the meeting to avoid unnecessary background noise. You can also mute your own microphone when not speaking.

- **How to Use**:
    - **Mute Yourself**: Click the microphone icon at the bottom of your screen to mute or unmute yourself. When muted, the icon will have a red slash through it.

    - **Mute All Participants**: Click on the "Participants" button in the toolbar. You'll see the list of attendees. From here, you can click "Mute All" to prevent everyone from speaking. You can also allow participants to unmute themselves if you choose.

Video/Stop Video:

- **Why It's Important**: Video is a powerful tool for connecting with your students and keeping the class dynamic. Showing your face can make the class feel more personal and interactive.

- **How to Use**:

  - **Turn Video On/Off**: The video icon is located in the bottom-left corner of the Zoom window. You can turn it on or off depending on your preference or if you need to step away momentarily.

  - **Virtual Backgrounds**: If you don't want your background to be distracting, you can use Zoom's virtual background feature. Go to **Settings > Background & Filters** and choose a pre-made background or upload your own.

Screen Sharing:

- **Why It's Important**: Sharing your screen allows you to present slides, documents, videos, or any other content that supports your lesson. This feature is indispensable for demonstrating concepts or guiding students through exercises.

- **How to Use**:

  - Click the **"Share Screen"** button located in the toolbar. You can choose to share your entire desktop or just one specific application (e.g., PowerPoint, a webpage, a video).

  - You can also share audio when sharing videos by selecting the **"Share computer sound"** option in the bottom-left corner of the screen-sharing window.

  - **Advanced Sharing Options**: You can limit screen-sharing permissions to yourself or allow others to share their screens, depending on your classroom needs.

2. Managing Participants: Mute All, Breakout Rooms, and More

Managing participants effectively is essential for creating a focused and orderly online class. Zoom offers several tools to help you stay in control of your meeting.

Mute All Participants:

- **Why It's Important**: In larger meetings, background noise can quickly become overwhelming. Muting all participants ensures that only the speaker is heard, keeping the focus on the lesson.

- **How to Use**:
  - Click on the **Participants** button in the toolbar. You'll see a list of attendees.
  - From the bottom of the participant list, click **"Mute All"**. You can also choose whether to allow participants to unmute themselves.

Breakout Rooms:

- **Why It's Important**: Breakout rooms allow you to divide your students into smaller groups for collaborative work or discussions. This is especially helpful for group projects, discussions, or peer review activities.

- **How to Use**:
  - Click on the **Breakout Rooms** button in the toolbar to start dividing your meeting into smaller groups.
  - Zoom will give you the option to either **manually** assign students to rooms or let Zoom **automatically** assign them based on the number of rooms you select.
  - Once the rooms are set up, you can click **"Open All Rooms"** to send participants to their assigned rooms.

- As the host, you can join any breakout room at any time to observe or assist students.

- To close the rooms, click **"Close All Rooms"**, and participants will return to the main meeting.

Managing Participants in Breakout Rooms:

- **Monitor Rooms**: You can visit individual breakout rooms to observe student interactions, provide guidance, or answer questions.

- **Broadcast a Message**: You can send a message to all breakout rooms simultaneously to remind students of time limits or provide additional instructions.

- **Move Participants**: If needed, you can manually move participants from one breakout room to another.

3. Using the Chat Function Effectively

The chat function is a great way to encourage student interaction, provide additional resources, and manage questions during class. Here's how you can use it effectively:

Sending Messages:

- **Public Chat**: This allows everyone in the meeting to see your message. Use it to share links, resources, or important reminders.

- **Private Chat**: You can send private messages to individual participants, which can be helpful for addressing concerns or giving feedback.

Managing Chat:

- **Enable/Disable Chat**: As the host, you can choose whether participants can chat with everyone or only with the host. This can be controlled in the settings, either for the entire meeting or for specific times (e.g., during a lecture or presentation).

- **Save Chat**: After the meeting, you can save the chat to review questions or feedback shared by your students. Simply click on the **"More"** button in the chat window and select **"Save Chat"**.

Using the Chat for Engagement:

- **Encourage Questions**: Ask students to type their questions in the chat if they are not comfortable speaking up.

- **Poll Responses**: You can use chat to collect feedback, for example, by asking students to type "yes" or "no" in response to a question, or you can create informal polls during the class.

4. Recording Your Meetings: Benefits and How-to

Recording your Zoom meetings allows students to revisit the content after the session. This is especially helpful for review, catching up on missed lessons, or reinforcing important concepts.

Benefits of Recording:

- **Student Access**: Students can go back and rewatch the session if they missed anything or need clarification.

- **Self-Reflection**: As a teacher, you can review your own lessons to identify areas of improvement, assess pacing, and refine your teaching methods.

- **Archiving**: Recordings serve as a valuable archive of your lessons that can be shared with other colleagues or used as future references.

How to Record:

1. **Start Recording**: While in a meeting, click on the **"Record"** button in the toolbar. You'll be given the option to record to your computer or the cloud (if you have a paid account).

2. **During the Meeting**: You can pause or stop the recording at any time. To resume, simply click the **"Record"** button again.

3. **End of Meeting**: Once the meeting ends, the recording will automatically save. If recorded locally, it will be saved on your

computer; if recorded to the cloud, you'll receive a link to access and share it.

4. **Sharing the Recording**: Once your recording is ready, you can share the link with your students or download the video for offline access.

5. Managing Screen Sharing and Whiteboard Tools

Zoom's screen-sharing feature is essential for displaying your content, and the whiteboard tool is perfect for real-time drawing and collaboration.

Managing Screen Sharing:

- **Start Screen Sharing**: Click on the **"Share Screen"** button in the toolbar. You'll be given the option to share your entire desktop or specific applications. This feature allows you to display slides, web pages, or documents, making your lesson more interactive and engaging.

- **Advanced Sharing Options**: You can also select whether or not to share your computer's audio if you're showing a video. Additionally, you can grant participants permission to share their screen.

- **Stop Screen Sharing**: When you're done, click the **"Stop Share"** button at the top of the screen to end the screen-sharing session.

Using the Whiteboard:

- **Starting the Whiteboard**: To use the whiteboard, click **"Share Screen"** and then select **"Whiteboard"** from the options. This will bring up a blank, digital canvas where you can draw, write, or annotate.

- **Annotating**: You can use the pen, highlighter, and text tools to add notes, explanations, or diagrams. Students can also be given permission to annotate the whiteboard, encouraging interaction.

- **Clearing the Whiteboard**: If needed, you can clear all annotations by clicking on the **"Clear"** button in the toolbar.

By mastering these essential features, you'll be able to engage your students more effectively, manage your online classroom with confidence, and create a dynamic and interactive virtual learning environment. In the next chapter, we'll explore advanced Zoom features and tips to further elevate your teaching experience.

Chapter 4: Engaging Your Students in Virtual Classes

One of the biggest challenges in online teaching is keeping your students actively engaged. Unlike in a traditional classroom where you can read body language and foster immediate interaction, virtual environments require creative tools and strategies to maintain attention and participation. In this chapter, we'll cover several key techniques for keeping your virtual students engaged, from polls and reactions to breakout rooms and annotation tools. Mastering these features will help you create a dynamic, interactive learning experience.

1. Polls and Reactions for Interactive Learning

Polls and reactions are simple yet effective ways to involve students in the lesson, gather feedback, and assess understanding during your Zoom sessions. These tools provide real-time interaction, making it easier to keep students involved and ensure they're following the material.

Polls:

- **Why They're Important**: Polls help you gauge student understanding and collect feedback quickly. They can also break up the flow of the lesson, providing a moment of active participation for your students.

- **How to Use Polls**:
    1. **Create a Poll Before the Meeting**:
        - Go to your Zoom account online and navigate to the **Meetings** tab.
        - Select your scheduled meeting, and scroll down to find the **Polls** section.

- Click **"Add a Poll"**, then enter your poll questions (multiple choice or single choice) and possible answers.

2. **Create a Poll During the Meeting**:

   - In your meeting, click **"Polls"** in the toolbar.

   - Click **"Add a Question"**, then enter your poll question and answers. You can ask things like, "How confident do you feel about today's material?" or "Which topic would you like to review again?"

3. **Launching the Poll**: When you're ready to ask your students, click **"Launch Poll"** to make it appear on their screens. Participants will vote, and you can see the results in real time.

4. **Review Results**: After the poll ends, click **"End Poll"** and share the results with your class. This provides transparency and allows you to adjust your teaching based on their responses.

Reactions:

- **Why They're Important**: Reactions are a non-verbal way for students to express their thoughts during the class, such as showing agreement, appreciation, or enthusiasm.

- **How to Use Reactions**:

  - In the Zoom toolbar, students can click the **"Reactions"** button to send emoticons like thumbs up, applause, or laughter.

  - As the teacher, encourage students to use reactions to show they're following along, celebrating moments of success, or reacting to something funny or insightful. This keeps the energy up and fosters a sense of community.

2. Creating Breakout Rooms for Group Work

Breakout rooms are a great way to divide your class into smaller groups, encouraging collaboration, problem-solving, and peer learning. This feature allows students to work together on assignments, discuss ideas, and engage more deeply with the material.

Why They're Important:

- **Interactive Learning**: Breakout rooms enable students to collaborate with their peers, fostering teamwork and critical thinking.

- **Small Group Discussions**: Some students may feel shy to speak in front of the whole class but are more comfortable participating in a smaller group. Breakout rooms give them a chance to share their ideas and ask questions.

- **Differentiated Instruction**: You can assign students to breakout rooms based on their needs, allowing for targeted instruction and more personalized learning experiences.

How to Use Breakout Rooms:

1. **Set Up Breakout Rooms Before the Meeting**:
   - Before your meeting, navigate to your **Zoom settings** and enable the **Breakout Rooms** feature (if it's not already enabled).
   - In the meeting, click **Breakout Rooms** in the toolbar to create your rooms. You can decide how many rooms you need and whether you want to assign students automatically or manually.

2. **Assign Students to Breakout Rooms**:
   - **Automatic**: Zoom can automatically assign participants to rooms based on the number of rooms you select.

- o **Manual**: You can manually assign students to specific rooms based on group work requirements or skill levels.

3. **Open the Rooms**: After setting up the rooms, click **"Open All Rooms"**. Students will be automatically moved to their assigned rooms, and you'll be able to join any room at any time.

4. **Monitor and Assist**: As the host, you can visit any breakout room to monitor discussions, answer questions, or provide additional guidance.

5. **Close the Rooms**: When the session is over, click **"Close All Rooms"** to bring students back to the main session.

Tips for Using Breakout Rooms Effectively:

- Set clear objectives for the group work so students know what is expected of them.

- Keep track of time. Set a timer to let students know when they should return to the main session.

- Give students an opportunity to share their breakout room discussions with the class when they reconvene.

3. Managing Discussions and Student Engagement

Encouraging active participation in a virtual classroom can be challenging, but with the right strategies, you can maintain an engaging and interactive environment.

Managing Discussions:

- **Encourage Student Interaction**: Ask open-ended questions that require more than just a "yes" or "no" answer. This encourages students to think critically and engage in meaningful discussions.

- **Use "Raise Hand" Feature**: In larger classes, use the **"Raise Hand"** feature to give students the opportunity to speak without interrupting. This allows you to manage discussions more easily and gives each student a chance to contribute.

- o To raise a hand, participants click **"Reactions"** and select the **"Raise Hand"** option.

- o As the host, you'll see a raised hand icon next to the participant's name, signaling they want to speak.

Tips for Keeping Students Engaged:

- **Interactive Questions**: Instead of just lecturing, ask students questions that require their input. You can use the **chat** function or **polls** for quick feedback.

- **Use Multimedia**: Share videos, infographics, or presentations to break up the monotony of text-based learning.

- **Gamify Lessons**: Incorporate quizzes or games into your teaching. This can be done using Zoom's polling feature or external tools like Kahoot! or Quizizz.

4. Using the Annotation Tool for Interactive Lessons

The annotation tool is a fantastic feature that allows you to draw, highlight, and write on shared content during your lesson. This can be a powerful way to emphasize key points, explain complex concepts, or engage students directly in the learning process.

Why It's Important:

- **Visual Learning**: Visual learners benefit from annotations, which help clarify ideas and make abstract concepts more concrete.

- **Collaboration**: Students can also use the annotation tool, which promotes collaboration and allows them to actively participate in lesson creation.

- **Engagement**: Instead of just passively viewing slides, students can interact with the content, making the lesson more dynamic.

How to Use the Annotation Tool:

1. **Share Your Screen**: Before you can use the annotation tool, you need to be sharing your screen. Once you share your screen, the

annotation tools will appear in a small toolbar at the top of the screen.

2. **Drawing Tools**: You can select from several drawing tools, including a pen, highlighter, and eraser. Use the pen to underline key points or draw diagrams, or use the highlighter to emphasize important areas of the screen.

3. **Text Tool**: The **Text** tool allows you to add text directly to the screen. This is useful for labeling parts of an image, writing questions, or adding short explanations.

4. **Shapes**: Use the shape tool to add circles, squares, arrows, or lines to your shared content. This is helpful for diagrams or when you want to point out something specific.

5. **Clear Annotations**: After the class, you can clear annotations by clicking **"Clear All Annotations"** or allow students to erase their own marks if they've interacted with the content.

Using Annotations with Students:

- **Collaborative Activities**: Assign students to annotate a shared document or slide as part of an activity. This encourages students to work together and share their ideas visually.

- **Interactive Brainstorming**: During discussions, ask students to use the annotation tools to share their thoughts directly on the screen. For example, they could circle the most important idea or highlight a quote that stood out to them.

By using these tools and techniques, you can create an engaging, dynamic virtual classroom that fosters participation, critical thinking, and active learning. Whether you're using polls to check understanding, breakout rooms for group work, or the annotation tool for interactive lessons, these features will help you make the most out of your Zoom sessions and keep your students engaged from start to finish.

Chapter 5: Troubleshooting Common Issues

Despite its powerful features, Zoom can occasionally present issues that disrupt the flow of your virtual classes. Knowing how to troubleshoot and resolve common problems ensures that your lessons run smoothly and that students stay engaged. In this chapter, we'll explore some of the most frequent issues you might encounter during a Zoom meeting, how to address them, and best practices for keeping your classes running seamlessly.

1. Solving Audio and Video Problems

Audio and video issues are among the most common problems encountered during Zoom meetings. These issues can disrupt communication, making it hard for students to follow along. Here's how to troubleshoot common audio and video problems:

Audio Problems:

1. **Check Your Microphone**:

    o **Ensure it's not muted**: The most common issue is simply that the microphone is muted. Check the **mute/unmute** icon in the bottom-left corner of the Zoom window.

    o **Test your microphone**: Click the **arrow** next to the microphone icon and select **Test Speaker & Microphone** to check whether your microphone is working properly.

    o **Check your input settings**: In the Zoom settings, go to **Audio** and ensure your desired microphone is selected as the input device. If using an external microphone or headset, make sure it's properly connected.

2. **Audio Echoes or Feedback:**

- o **Use headphones**: If you hear feedback or echoing sounds, have participants use headphones to prevent their microphone from picking up sound from the speakers.

- o **Mute other participants**: In a larger class, if multiple people are unmuted at once, audio feedback can occur. Use the **Mute All** option to reduce this issue.

3. **Participants Can't Hear You**:

- o **Check volume settings**: Ensure the volume on your computer or device is set to an appropriate level.

- o **Rejoin the meeting**: If the problem persists, try leaving and rejoining the meeting to reset your audio connection.

Video Problems:

1. **Video Not Working**:

- o **Ensure video is enabled**: Click the **Start Video** button in the bottom-left corner of the Zoom window. If it's already clicked, toggle it off and on again to reset it.

- o **Check your camera**: Make sure your camera is properly connected if you're using an external webcam. You can check your camera settings in Zoom by clicking the **Settings** icon, selecting **Video**, and testing the camera.

- o **Update drivers**: If your camera is not working, ensure your camera's drivers are up to date, especially if you're using an external webcam.

2. **Low Video Quality**:

- o **Enable HD video**: In the **Video settings**, enable **HD video** to improve the quality of your video feed.

- o **Check your internet speed**: Low bandwidth can affect video quality. Consider switching to a more stable internet connection or lowering the video quality to **Standard Definition (SD)** in your Zoom settings.

3. **Video Freezing**:

   o **Close unnecessary programs**: If your computer is running too many applications, it can slow down the video feed. Close any unnecessary programs to free up processing power.

   o **Check for software updates**: Ensure your Zoom app and your device's operating system are up to date to avoid compatibility issues.

2. Managing Connectivity Issues

Connectivity problems, such as lagging, freezing, or difficulty joining a meeting, can be incredibly frustrating. Here's how to troubleshoot these common internet-related issues:

Lagging or Freezing:

1. **Check your internet speed**:

   o **Test your connection**: Run a speed test (e.g., Speedtest.net) to determine if your internet speed is sufficient for video conferencing. Zoom recommends a minimum download speed of 1.5 Mbps for high-quality video.

   o **Switch to a wired connection**: If possible, use an Ethernet cable to connect to the internet. Wired connections are generally more stable than Wi-Fi.

   o **Lower video quality**: In Zoom's **Settings**, under **Video**, you can reduce the video resolution to **Standard Definition (SD)** or disable HD video to reduce bandwidth usage.

2. **Reduce Background Processes**:

- **Close other applications**: Streaming videos, large downloads, or other heavy applications can consume bandwidth and processing power. Close unnecessary programs during the meeting to free up resources.

3. **Switch Devices**:

- If the issue persists, try switching devices. If you're using a laptop, try joining from a desktop, or use a mobile device if available.

Difficulty Joining a Meeting:

1. **Check the Meeting Link and Password**:

- Ensure the meeting link you received is correct and that you have the correct meeting ID and password (if applicable).

2. **Update the Zoom App**:

- Sometimes, joining issues are caused by outdated Zoom versions. Check for updates within the Zoom app or download the latest version from the Zoom website.

3. **Reinstall Zoom**:

- If other solutions don't work, try uninstalling and reinstalling Zoom to resolve any corrupted files or settings.

3. Handling Participant Challenges

Sometimes, students may experience technical difficulties or exhibit behaviors that interfere with the flow of the class. Here's how to handle some common participant-related challenges:

Disruptive Participants:

1. **Mute Participants**: If a participant is being disruptive with background noise, you can mute them either individually or use the **Mute All** feature to silence everyone upon entry.

2. **Use the Waiting Room**: Before the meeting begins, you can enable the **Waiting Room** feature, which lets you screen participants before allowing them to enter the class. This is useful for preventing unwanted guests or ensuring that only students are joining the meeting.

3. **Remove Participants**: If someone is repeatedly disruptive or violating meeting rules, you can remove them from the meeting. Click on the **Participants** button, find the participant's name, click **More**, and select **Remove**.

4. **Lock the Meeting**: To prevent new participants from joining, you can lock the meeting once all attendees have arrived. Click **Participants**, then **Lock Meeting**.

Students Struggling with Technology:

1. **Offer Technical Assistance**: Sometimes, students may have trouble with their microphone, camera, or screen-sharing settings. Offer a brief tutorial at the start of class to ensure they understand how to use basic features.

2. **Provide Written Instructions**: Before class, send out instructions on how to join the meeting, turn on audio/video, and troubleshoot common problems. This can help alleviate confusion, especially for less tech-savvy students.

3. **Test Your Tech in Advance**: Encourage students to test their equipment before the meeting begins. This minimizes the chances of disruptions during the session.

4. Keeping Your Classes Running Smoothly

The key to a successful Zoom class is proactive preparation and maintaining a smooth workflow during the session. Here are a few best practices to keep things running without a hitch:

Prepare in Advance:

1. **Check Equipment**: Before your class begins, test your audio, video, and screen-sharing settings. Make sure everything is working properly.

2. **Have a Backup Plan**: Be prepared for any tech issues by having a backup plan. For instance, keep a phone handy in case your internet connection fails or consider using a second device as a backup for teaching if necessary.

3. **Keep a Structured Agenda**: Ensure that your lessons are well-planned and that you stick to the schedule. Having a clear agenda helps prevent disruptions and keeps the class focused.

Set Ground Rules:

1. **Set Expectations for Participation**: At the beginning of each session, set expectations for student behavior. Remind students to mute themselves when not speaking, use the chat function for questions, and raise their hands if they want to speak.

2. **Use the Waiting Room**: To avoid interruptions at the start of your class, use the **Waiting Room** feature to let students in only when you're ready.

Monitor Engagement:

1. **Use Breakout Rooms for Small-Group Activities**: If you're teaching a large class, break it down into smaller groups using breakout rooms. This allows students to engage more effectively, collaborate, and share ideas.

2. **Use Polls and Reactions**: Incorporate interactive features like polls and reactions to encourage participation. Regular use of these tools can keep students engaged and give you valuable feedback on their understanding.

Follow Up After Class:

1. **Provide Recordings**: After the meeting, share a recording of the class, along with any supplementary materials. This gives

students a chance to review the content and catch up if they missed anything.

2. **Send a Summary or Feedback Form**: Send a brief summary of the session or ask for student feedback. This helps you identify areas of improvement and ensures students know what to focus on for the next class.

By being prepared to handle common issues and keeping your classroom running smoothly, you'll create a positive and productive virtual environment for your students. These troubleshooting skills and proactive strategies will help you manage any technical hiccups that may arise and ensure that your classes continue without interruptions.

Chapter 6: Advanced Zoom Features for Online Educators

Once you've mastered the basics of Zoom, it's time to explore some of the more advanced features that can elevate your online teaching experience. In this chapter, we will dive into the options that allow you to host recurring meetings, customize your virtual classroom environment, integrate Zoom with Learning Management Systems (LMS), and explore third-party integrations. These advanced features provide you with the tools to create more professional, organized, and interactive online learning experiences.

1. Setting Up Recurring Meetings and Webinar Options

As an online educator, you may want to run regular classes or events. Zoom makes it easy to set up recurring meetings and webinars for ongoing sessions, ensuring consistency and ease of access for your students.

Setting Up Recurring Meetings:

- **Why It's Important**: Recurring meetings are perfect for weekly or daily classes, as they allow students to use the same link for every session. This is especially useful for ongoing courses, study groups, or tutoring sessions.

How to Set Up a Recurring Meeting:

1. **Schedule a Meeting**: Go to your Zoom dashboard or app, and click **Schedule a New Meeting**.

2. **Set Recurrence**: In the scheduling window, check the box for **"Recurring Meeting"**.

3. **Choose Frequency**: You can choose to have the meeting repeat daily, weekly, monthly, or at custom intervals. You can also set the start date and the end date (e.g., end after a certain number of occurrences or after a specific date).

4. **Save**: Once you've filled in the other meeting details (like time, passcode, and video settings), click **Save**. The meeting link remains the same for each occurrence, making it easy for students to join future sessions.

Webinar Options:

- **Why It's Important**: Webinars allow you to host large sessions with up to 1,000 participants, which is perfect for lectures, presentations, or guest speakers. Webinars have specialized features like attendee registration, Q&A, and the ability to limit interactions to host-only.

How to Set Up a Webinar:

1. **Access Webinar Settings**: Webinars are available with a Zoom webinar license. If you don't have this license, you'll need to purchase one.

2. **Schedule Your Webinar**: Once you have the webinar license, go to your Zoom dashboard and click **Schedule a Webinar**.

3. **Set Webinar Details**: Similar to scheduling meetings, you'll need to set the webinar's date, time, and other settings, such as whether you want to enable Q&A or allow attendees to view each other.

4. **Send Invitations**: Once set up, you can send webinar invitations with the link to the event, much like you would for regular meetings. You can also enable **Registration** to collect attendee information before they can join the webinar.

2. Customizing Your Virtual Classroom Environment

Your virtual classroom environment is the space where learning happens. Customizing this environment can make your classes feel more engaging, professional, and tailored to your teaching style. Zoom offers several options to create a personalized classroom experience.

Virtual Backgrounds and Filters:

- **Why It's Important**: Virtual backgrounds allow you to replace your real background with an image or video of your choice. This can create a more professional atmosphere, reduce distractions, or just add fun to your classroom.

How to Use Virtual Backgrounds:

1. **Choose or Upload Backgrounds**: Go to **Settings > Background & Filters** in the Zoom app. You can select one of the preloaded backgrounds or upload your own custom images or videos.

2. **Lighting and Quality**: Make sure your lighting is good enough for the virtual background to work smoothly. Poor lighting can make the background look glitchy or create a "floating head" effect.

Touch Up My Appearance:

- **Why It's Important**: The **Touch Up My Appearance** feature subtly smooths out your video feed, giving you a polished, professional look. This can be particularly useful if you're recording classes for later viewing.

How to Enable It:

1. Go to **Settings > Video > Touch Up My Appearance** and toggle the option on.

Customizing Meeting Layouts:

- **Why It's Important**: A customized layout allows you to focus on the content being shared or make the gallery view more engaging.

How to Customize Layouts:

- **Speaker View**: This view highlights the speaker, making it ideal for lectures and presentations.

- Gallery View: This shows all participants in a grid format and is great for discussions or group activities.

- Hide Non-Video Participants: You can choose to hide participants who have their video off. This keeps the focus on the active participants.

- Pin or Spotlight Video: You can pin a specific participant's video (including your own) to ensure their video feed stays visible. Spotlighting can be used to highlight a specific speaker or presenter during the session.

3. Using Zoom with Other Learning Platforms (LMS)

Zoom integrates seamlessly with many Learning Management Systems (LMS), such as Canvas, Moodle, Blackboard, and Google Classroom. This integration streamlines the process of scheduling, attending, and recording Zoom sessions directly from within your LMS.

Why It's Important:

- Centralized Learning Experience: Integration between Zoom and your LMS allows students to access all course materials, discussions, and Zoom meetings in one place, creating a more cohesive and organized learning environment.

- Ease of Scheduling: Teachers can schedule Zoom sessions directly from the LMS, and students can join with a single click.

How to Integrate Zoom with Your LMS:

1. Canvas Integration:

   - Go to your Canvas course and select Zoom from the course navigation menu.

   - Click Schedule a New Meeting, and set up your meeting as usual. Zoom will automatically add it to your Canvas course calendar.

2. Google Classroom Integration:

- You can share your Zoom meeting links directly within Google Classroom by adding the meeting link to the **Classwork** section, or by using third-party integrations like Google Meet or other add-ons.

3. **Moodle Integration**:

   - From the Moodle dashboard, navigate to the **Zoom plugin**. Here, you can schedule meetings, view past sessions, and share the meeting link with students directly in the Moodle platform.

4. **Blackboard Integration**:

   - In Blackboard, you can use the **Zoom Tool** to integrate Zoom directly into your course content. This enables easy meeting scheduling and management within Blackboard.

4. Exploring Third-Party Zoom Integrations for Teaching

In addition to the native LMS integrations, Zoom can also be enhanced with third-party tools to further improve the virtual learning experience. These integrations offer additional features that support collaboration, engagement, and content sharing.

Third-Party Integrations:

- **Google Drive**: Share and collaborate on documents in real-time during your Zoom session. This is useful for group activities or live document editing.

  - **How to Integrate**: Use the **Google Drive** integration to easily share files, presentations, or links with your students during a meeting.

- **Kahoot!**: Make your lessons more interactive by using Kahoot! quizzes in real-time during your Zoom sessions. This is an engaging way to assess students' understanding of the material.

- **How to Integrate**: Launch Kahoot! quizzes from your browser while using Zoom and share your screen to engage students in live polling or quizzes.

- **Padlet**: Use Padlet to create interactive boards where students can collaborate in real time by posting images, links, and text.

  - **How to Integrate**: Share your Padlet board with students during Zoom, and encourage them to add their contributions directly.

- **Slido**: For interactive Q&A sessions and live polls, Slido can be used to collect real-time feedback, ideas, or questions from students during class.

  - **How to Integrate**: Use Slido alongside your Zoom meeting by sharing the link to your Slido event in the Zoom chat. Students can ask questions or answer polls directly in Slido.

- **Trello**: Organize class activities, assignments, and projects with Trello boards, which you can share during Zoom meetings to keep everyone on track.

  - **How to Integrate**: Share your Trello board on Zoom by screen sharing, allowing students to collaborate and track their tasks.

Exploring Zoom Marketplace:

The **Zoom App Marketplace** has a wide range of integrations specifically designed for education. You can browse apps that integrate Zoom with tools for assessment, content sharing, gamification, and more.

- **How to Explore**: Visit the **Zoom App Marketplace**, search for "Education" apps, and explore the available third-party apps that you can integrate into your Zoom meetings. Many of these apps are free or offer educational discounts.

By mastering these advanced features, you can create a more organized, interactive, and professional learning experience for your students. Whether you're setting up recurring meetings, integrating Zoom with your LMS, or exploring third-party tools, these capabilities will help you stay ahead of the curve and make the most of your online teaching.

Chapter 7: Best Practices for Effective Online Teaching with Zoom

Online teaching requires careful planning, thoughtful structuring, and active engagement to ensure that students are not only learning but staying motivated throughout the course. Zoom, as a versatile tool, provides you with the platform to create dynamic, interactive, and organized online classes. In this chapter, we'll cover best practices that will help you optimize your virtual teaching environment and maximize your students' learning experiences.

1. Planning Your Virtual Class Ahead of Time

Proper planning is the foundation of any successful online class. Being well-prepared helps ensure that everything runs smoothly and that you can maintain focus on delivering valuable content. Here's how to plan effectively:

Why It's Important:

- **Reduces Stress**: Having a clear plan minimizes last-minute issues and ensures you're ready for anything that might arise during class.

- **Improves Organization**: Planning ahead ensures that your class is structured, well-paced, and focused on achieving specific learning goals.

- **Saves Time**: Efficient planning allows you to make the most of your teaching time and avoid wasting valuable minutes troubleshooting or figuring things out on the fly.

How to Plan:

1. **Set Clear Learning Objectives**: Before your class, define the key takeaways you want your students to have by the end of the session. These objectives should be measurable, such as "By

the end of this class, students will be able to solve quadratic equations" or "Students will understand the key concepts of supply and demand."

2. **Prepare Materials and Resources**: Make sure all your content (slides, documents, videos, etc.) is ready and easily accessible. Upload resources to a shared platform (e.g., Google Drive, Moodle, or Canvas) or directly into Zoom via the **"Files"** tab for easy access during the meeting.

3. **Check Technology**: Ensure that your equipment is functioning properly—test your microphone, camera, and internet connection. Familiarize yourself with Zoom's features, such as screen sharing, breakout rooms, and the chat function, to ensure you can navigate the platform without disruption.

4. **Communicate with Students**: Send out any materials, links, or expectations ahead of time. This might include readings, assignments, or instructions on how to join the class. Let students know what tools or platforms they'll be using and encourage them to test their technology beforehand.

2. Creating a Structured and Engaging Lesson Plan

A well-structured lesson plan is essential for maintaining a productive and engaging virtual classroom. Online learners need structure, especially given the distractions of remote learning, so creating a plan that balances content delivery, student interaction, and active learning is key.

Why It's Important:

- **Keeps the Class Focused**: A clear lesson plan ensures that you stay on track and cover all necessary material.

- **Promotes Active Learning**: Incorporating diverse activities into your plan helps keep students engaged and encourages participation.

- **Maximizes Time**: With a structured plan, you'll make the best use of the class time, keeping students focused on the topic without feeling rushed or lost.

How to Create a Structured Plan:

1. **Introduction (5-10 minutes):**

   o Start with a brief overview of what you'll be covering in the session and the key objectives.

   o Make a connection with your students by asking them how they're doing or engaging them with a quick icebreaker activity to set the tone for the session.

2. **Lecture/Presentation (15-20 minutes):**

   o Use your slides or visuals to explain key concepts. Focus on a few key points, ensuring that your explanation is clear and concise.

   o Avoid overwhelming students with too much content in one go. Break up the information into manageable chunks.

3. **Interactive Activity (10-15 minutes):**

   o After presenting key concepts, engage your students with an interactive activity such as a poll, quiz, group discussion, or brainstorming session. Zoom's **Breakout Rooms**, **Polling**, and **Whiteboard** tools are excellent for this.

4. **Group Work or Collaboration (10-15 minutes):**

   o Use **Breakout Rooms** to split students into small groups for collaborative exercises, discussions, or problem-solving tasks. Ensure each group has a clear objective to work on, and provide guidance as needed.

5. **Q&A and Wrap-Up (5-10 minutes):**

o End the session by inviting questions, reviewing the key takeaways, and providing any additional resources or homework. This is a good time to gather feedback from students and ensure they understand the material.

3. Maintaining Student Engagement and Focus

In an online setting, maintaining student engagement and focus can be challenging, as distractions are abundant. It's crucial to keep your students actively involved throughout the session.

Why It's Important:

- **Increases Learning Retention**: Engaged students are more likely to retain the information you present and be motivated to continue learning.

- **Prevents Distractions**: When students are engaged, they are less likely to check their phones, multitask, or lose focus.

- **Fosters a Positive Classroom Environment**: An interactive, engaging class encourages a sense of community and participation, even in a virtual environment.

How to Maintain Engagement:

1. **Use Interactive Features**:

   o **Polls**: Use Zoom's poll feature to ask questions related to the material you just covered. It's an effective way to gauge student understanding and encourage participation.

   o **Reactions**: Encourage students to use the "thumbs up" or other reactions to indicate agreement or understanding, which fosters a sense of connection and feedback.

2. **Break up the Lecture**:

   o **Keep it short and dynamic**: Don't let your lecture last more than 20 minutes without some form of interaction.

Break up your lecture into shorter segments to maintain focus.

- o **Ask Questions**: Involve students by asking questions throughout the session, prompting them to respond via audio, chat, or even with a poll. This keeps them attentive and actively thinking.

3. **Utilize Breakout Rooms**:

- o **Collaborative Activities**: Give students a chance to work in groups using breakout rooms. Encourage them to discuss key concepts, answer questions, or solve problems together. This helps students feel more connected and invested in the learning process.

4. **Use Visual and Multimedia Tools**:

- o **Incorporate videos, images, and diagrams** into your presentation to break up the monotony of text and engage different learning styles.

- o **Live demonstrations**: If applicable, demonstrate concepts live, using the **Whiteboard** or **Screen Share** to show practical examples or guide students through exercises.

5. **Be Energetic and Enthusiastic**:

- o Your energy and enthusiasm as the instructor will naturally encourage students to stay engaged. Smile, show interest in the material, and vary your tone to keep the class dynamic.

4. Handling Online Class Etiquette and Professionalism

Just like in a physical classroom, online classes require a level of professionalism and respect from both the instructor and students. Establishing clear guidelines around etiquette and communication helps ensure a smooth and respectful learning environment.

Why It's Important:

- **Maintains Professionalism**: Setting expectations for behavior helps to maintain a respectful and orderly learning environment.

- **Promotes Respectful Interaction**: Encouraging students to participate appropriately fosters mutual respect between the teacher and the students.

- **Ensures Class Focus**: Proper etiquette helps minimize distractions and ensures that the session remains productive.

How to Maintain Etiquette and Professionalism:

1. **Set Expectations for Behavior**:

   o At the beginning of your class, clearly outline expectations for student behavior. Remind them to mute themselves when not speaking, use the chat responsibly, and raise their hands if they want to speak.

2. **Professional Appearance**:

   o Dress appropriately for class, as you would in a physical classroom. Encourage students to do the same, creating a professional environment for learning.

3. **Avoid Interruptions**:

   o Encourage students to keep their cameras on if possible, as this helps reduce distractions and ensures they're actively participating. However, be mindful of students who may have limited bandwidth or other issues that make using video difficult.

4. **Respectful Communication**:

   o Remind students to use respectful language when communicating through audio, chat, or video. Online classrooms are diverse, so fostering an atmosphere of inclusivity and respect is vital.

5. **Monitor the Chat and Other Channels**:

o   Actively monitor the chat for questions, comments, and any issues that arise. If students are having technical difficulties, respond promptly. It's also important to address any inappropriate behavior in a timely manner.

By following these best practices, you can create a highly effective, organized, and engaging virtual classroom. Planning ahead, structuring your lessons well, maintaining student engagement, and enforcing professional etiquette will make your online teaching sessions more successful and enjoyable for both you and your students.

Conclusion

As we wrap up this guide on using Zoom for online teaching, it's important to reflect on the key takeaways and consider how to continue evolving as an educator in a digital space. Zoom is a powerful tool for fostering interaction, engagement, and collaboration in virtual classrooms, but like any platform, its full potential is unlocked through intentional use, practice, and continuous learning. In this conclusion, we'll summarize the key points from the book, explore how you can continue your online teaching journey, and discuss the next steps for mastering Zoom.

1. Key Takeaways for Zoom Success

By now, you should be equipped with a solid foundation of knowledge to host and manage Zoom meetings effectively. Here are the most important takeaways to help you succeed in your online teaching:

- **Preparation is Key**: Planning your virtual classes in advance—setting clear objectives, preparing materials, and testing your technology—ensures a smooth and organized session.

- **Mastering Zoom's Core Features**: Understanding and using key features like **Mute/Unmute**, **Video Settings**, **Screen Sharing**, **Breakout Rooms**, and **Polls** will enhance your ability to engage students and maintain control during your classes.

- **Interactivity Drives Engagement**: Incorporating features like **polls**, **Q&A sessions**, **breakout rooms**, and **annotations** will make your sessions more dynamic and keep students engaged, reducing distractions and boosting learning retention.

- **Security is Essential**: Protecting your meetings with features like **Waiting Rooms**, **Passwords**, and **Locking Meetings** ensures that only invited students can join, safeguarding both the learning environment and your privacy.

- **Structured Lessons for Online Learning**: A structured, engaging lesson plan with clear objectives, interactive moments, and time for student input fosters a productive and focused class environment.

- **Troubleshooting**: Know how to address common technical issues, such as **audio/video problems**, **connectivity issues**, and **disruptions from participants**, so that you can handle challenges calmly and keep your class running smoothly.

With these fundamental principles in place, you'll be well on your way to creating an effective, engaging, and secure online classroom with Zoom.

2. Continuing Your Online Teaching Journey

The shift to online teaching is not just a trend—it's a new way of delivering education that will likely continue to evolve. As an educator, you can embrace this shift as an opportunity for growth, creativity, and new approaches to teaching. Here's how to continue building on the foundation you've established:

- **Expand Your Digital Toolbox**: Zoom is just one part of the online teaching puzzle. Explore other tools and platforms—such as Google Classroom, Padlet, or interactive quizzes—that can complement Zoom and enhance your virtual classroom experience. Combining different technologies will help you create a more holistic and engaging learning environment.

- **Engage in Professional Development**: Stay updated with Zoom's new features and enhancements by exploring their educational resources, webinars, and help center. Participating in online communities and forums for educators can also provide valuable insights into best practices and creative ways to use Zoom.

- **Solicit Feedback from Students**: To improve your teaching methods, regularly ask your students for feedback on the virtual learning experience. Their input can help you identify areas for improvement and adjust your approach based on their needs. Use surveys or informal discussions at the end of classes to gather this information.

- **Experiment with Teaching Styles**: Online teaching offers more flexibility than traditional classrooms. Experiment with different formats, such as flipped classrooms, guest speakers, or project-based learning, to find what works best for your students and the content you're teaching.

- **Develop a Personal Connection with Students**: Even in an online setting, it's essential to foster meaningful connections with your students. Encourage open communication, show genuine interest in their progress, and provide personalized feedback. This will help maintain a supportive and positive virtual classroom atmosphere.

3. Next Steps for Mastering Zoom

Mastering Zoom requires more than just understanding its basic features. As you continue using Zoom for online teaching, there are several next steps you can take to refine your skills and maximize the platform's potential:

1. **Explore Advanced Zoom Features**:

   - Familiarize yourself with **Zoom webinars, advanced breakout room features**, and **customizable meeting settings**. These features can help you scale your teaching and create more interactive and professional online events.

   - Practice using advanced tools such as **live transcription, whiteboard annotations**, and **integration with external platforms** to enhance your presentations and engage your students.

2. **Attend Zoom Training and Webinars**:

   - Zoom offers a wide range of free and paid training options to help educators sharpen their skills. Participating in these training sessions will give you deeper insights into the platform's capabilities and allow you to stay updated on new features.

3. **Join Online Teaching Communities:**

   o Engaging with fellow online educators in communities such as Zoom's Educator Network, social media groups, or forums like Reddit and Facebook can provide valuable advice, teaching strategies, and inspiration for enhancing your classes.

4. **Invest in Higher-Quality Equipment:**

   o To improve the overall quality of your online classes, consider upgrading your equipment. A good microphone, webcam, lighting setup, and noise-canceling headphones will significantly enhance the teaching and learning experience.

5. **Use Analytics and Reporting:**

   o As you progress with Zoom, you can start using **Zoom's analytics and reporting features** to track student participation and engagement levels. Reviewing these reports will give you insights into which aspects of your class need more attention and how well students are absorbing the material.

6. **Record and Review Your Classes:**

   o Recording your sessions allows you to review your teaching style and delivery. You can analyze how you present the material, engage with students, and whether the pacing is effective. This self-reflection is an important step in improving as an online educator.

By taking these next steps, you can continue to improve your proficiency with Zoom and further enhance your online teaching skills. The world of online education is constantly evolving, and with the right mindset and tools, you can stay ahead of the curve and create an enriching learning experience for your students.

Final Thoughts

Whether you're teaching a small group of students or leading large, interactive classes, Zoom offers powerful tools to create a connected and engaging learning environment. The knowledge and strategies outlined in this book should serve as a foundation for your teaching journey, but remember that the most important aspect of teaching is your connection with your students. Keep experimenting with new tools, stay curious, and always look for ways to improve. With Zoom, you have the power to make learning both effective and enjoyable—your journey as an online educator has only just begun!

Book 2 - Google Classroom for Beginners

Introduction

As the digital transformation of education continues, online learning platforms have become essential tools for teachers. **Google Classroom** is one of the most popular and accessible platforms for organizing and delivering online education. Whether you're teaching in a hybrid environment, running a fully online class, or even incorporating technology into your traditional classroom, Google Classroom offers the flexibility, simplicity, and features you need to create an engaging learning experience. In this introduction, we will explore what Google Classroom is, how it compares to traditional classrooms, and what core features it offers to make teaching more efficient. We'll also outline how this guide will help you navigate and master Google Classroom, allowing you to fully harness its potential for your students.

1. What is Google Classroom and Why It's Great for Teachers

Google Classroom is a free, web-based platform developed by Google that simplifies the process of managing and organizing digital learning. It acts as a central hub for teachers to create assignments, provide feedback, and facilitate communication with students in a structured and organized manner. Google Classroom is designed to streamline the day-to-day tasks of teaching, such as distributing assignments, grading, and communicating with students, all while saving time and reducing the use of paper.

Why It's Great for Teachers:

- **User-Friendly Interface**: Google Classroom is simple to set up and easy to use, which means teachers can focus on teaching rather than technology. You don't need to be a tech expert to take full advantage of its features.

- **Integration with Google Apps**: Classroom seamlessly integrates with other Google Workspace apps, such as Google Docs, Google Sheets, Google Slides, and Google Drive. This allows for easy sharing of documents, collaboration, and file storage—all in one place.

- **Time-Saving Features**: With features like assignment grading, automated notifications, and a streamlined grading system, Google Classroom saves teachers time by organizing everything in one easy-to-navigate platform.

- **Collaboration**: Google Classroom fosters collaborative learning by allowing students to work together on projects, share resources, and discuss materials. Teachers can also provide feedback directly on assignments in real-time, helping to maintain continuous communication with students.

- **Accessibility**: Because it's a cloud-based platform, Google Classroom is accessible from any device with internet access. This makes it easy for students to join the class, complete assignments, and stay connected—whether they're at home, at school, or on the go.

2. Google Classroom vs. Traditional Classrooms: Benefits of Digital Learning

While traditional classrooms have been the cornerstone of education for centuries, digital learning platforms like Google Classroom offer several advantages that support both teachers and students in today's fast-paced, technology-driven world. The transition to online learning provides flexibility, more efficient communication, and improved engagement.

Benefits Over Traditional Classrooms:

- **Remote Learning**: Google Classroom supports remote learning, allowing students to access assignments, lectures, and materials from anywhere. This becomes especially important in situations where in-person learning isn't possible, such as during snow days, emergencies, or when teaching students in different geographical locations.

- **Centralized Organization**: Unlike traditional classrooms where assignments might be scattered across papers or different tools, Google Classroom centralizes everything—assignments, grades, announcements, and feedback—into one easily accessible platform. This organization makes it easier for teachers to keep track of student progress and for students to stay on top of their work.

- **Instant Feedback and Grading**: In a traditional classroom, grading can be time-consuming, and feedback may take a while to reach students. Google Classroom allows teachers to provide instant feedback on assignments and grade them efficiently. Automated features, such as grade calculations and assignment tracking, further reduce the administrative burden on teachers.

- **Student Engagement**: Google Classroom fosters greater engagement by incorporating multimedia and interactive elements. Teachers can upload videos, create interactive assignments, and use Google Meet for live virtual classes. This interactive environment can help make learning more exciting for students.

- **Customization for Diverse Learning Needs**: Digital platforms like Google Classroom can be customized to fit different teaching styles and learning needs. You can use various teaching resources, tools, and assignments that cater to the specific needs of your students, whether it's creating a self-paced learning environment or offering additional resources for students who need extra help.

- **Environmental Impact**: By moving away from paper-based assignments, tests, and communication, Google Classroom is a more sustainable solution for schools. Reducing paper usage not only saves costs but also supports eco-friendly practices in education.

3. An Overview of Google Classroom's Core Features

Google Classroom comes with a host of features designed to streamline the teaching process and enhance the learning experience. Here's a quick overview of the core features that make it an ideal platform for both teachers and students:

Core Features:

1. **Classroom Stream:**

   o The **Stream** is the main communication hub for your class. It's where you can post announcements, share updates, and provide important information to your students. Students can also interact here by posting questions or comments.

2. **Assignments:**

   o The **Assignments** feature allows you to create and distribute assignments with ease. You can attach documents, set due dates, and provide clear instructions. Students can complete and submit their assignments directly through the platform. You can then grade and provide feedback right on the assignment itself.

3. **Gradebook:**

   o The **Gradebook** automatically organizes all student submissions and allows teachers to grade assignments directly in Google Classroom. You can easily track student progress, see grades, and maintain a record of students' work over time.

4. **Google Drive Integration:**

   o Google Classroom integrates seamlessly with **Google Drive,** allowing teachers and students to easily share and store files. Teachers can share folders or individual documents with students, and students can upload their work directly to the platform.

5. **Google Meet Integration**:

   o Google Classroom integrates with **Google Meet**, allowing you to schedule and host live virtual classes or meetings with students. You can share the Google Meet link directly in the Classroom stream, making it simple for students to join.

6. **Announcements and Notifications**:

   o You can create announcements to share important class updates, reminders, or changes with your students. Students will receive automatic notifications for new assignments, upcoming deadlines, and any announcements you post.

7. **Collaboration Tools**:

   o Google Classroom allows students to collaborate on assignments through **Google Docs, Sheets, and Slides**. Teachers can also enable collaborative spaces for group work, where students can interact and edit documents in real time.

8. **Calendar**:

   o Google Classroom syncs with **Google Calendar**, allowing both teachers and students to keep track of assignment deadlines, class events, and virtual meetings. This ensures that everyone stays organized and aware of upcoming tasks.

9. **Accessibility Features**:

   o Google Classroom includes accessibility features like screen readers, closed captioning, and language translation tools, making it more inclusive for students with diverse learning needs.

4. How This Guide Will Help You Set Up and Master Google Classroom

This guide is designed to help you navigate the world of Google Classroom, from setting up your account to mastering all the features it offers. Whether you're a first-time user or looking to enhance your current knowledge, this guide will provide you with practical, step-by-step instructions and best practices to ensure that your experience with Google Classroom is smooth and successful.

What You'll Learn in This Guide:

- **Setting Up Your Google Classroom**: From creating your first class to organizing your materials, we'll walk you through the process of setting up Google Classroom to suit your teaching needs.

- **Creating and Managing Assignments**: Learn how to create assignments, set deadlines, provide feedback, and grade work using Google Classroom's simple yet powerful tools.

- **Organizing Your Class Effectively**: Discover how to use the **Stream**, **Classwork**, and **Grades** tabs to organize your class materials and communicate efficiently with your students.

- **Best Practices for Student Engagement**: Learn how to use Google Classroom's features to keep your students engaged and motivated, whether through interactive assignments, group work, or live sessions.

- **Troubleshooting and Troubleshooting Tips**: We'll cover common issues teachers might encounter with Google Classroom and provide tips on how to solve them quickly.

By the end of this guide, you'll be well on your way to mastering Google Classroom, creating a more organized, interactive, and effective learning experience for both you and your students.

Google Classroom offers a wealth of opportunities for educators to enhance the learning experience and streamline administrative tasks. Whether you're just getting started or looking to refine your teaching process, this guide will provide you with the tools and knowledge you need to make the most of Google Classroom in your teaching practice. Let's dive in and start mastering the platform!

Chapter 1: Setting Up Google Classroom

Getting started with Google Classroom is straightforward, but setting it up properly can make a big difference in how smoothly your online teaching goes. In this chapter, we'll guide you through creating your Google Classroom account, navigating the dashboard, setting up your first class, and organizing your classroom to ensure success. By the end of this chapter, you'll be ready to start using Google Classroom with confidence and efficiency.

1. Creating Your Google Classroom Account

Before you can use Google Classroom, you need a Google account. If you already have a Google account (Gmail), you can easily set up Google Classroom using that account. Here's how to create and set up your account:

Steps to Create a Google Classroom Account:

1. **Sign in to Google**: Go to www.google.com and sign in to your existing Google account. If you don't have one, you can easily create one by clicking **Create Account** and following the prompts.

2. **Access Google Classroom**:

    o   Open your web browser and go to Google Classroom.

    o   If this is your first time using Google Classroom, you will be prompted to accept the terms and conditions. Click **Accept** to move forward.

3. **Join or Create a Class**:

    o   After accepting the terms, you'll be taken to your **Google Classroom dashboard**. Here you'll see options to either join an existing class (if you're a student) or create a new class (if you're a teacher).

- o Since you're setting up as a teacher, click the **"+"** icon in the top-right corner and select **Create Class**.

4. **Enter Class Details:**

   - o You'll be prompted to fill in basic details about your class:

      - ▪ **Class Name**: Choose a clear and descriptive name for your class (e.g., "Math 101" or "English Literature - Spring 2025").

      - ▪ **Section** (optional): If your class has multiple sections or periods, you can specify this here.

      - ▪ **Subject**: Choose the subject area that best fits your class.

      - ▪ **Room** (optional): You can leave this blank or input a physical room number if applicable.

   - o Once you've filled out the information, click **Create**.

Now your Google Classroom account is set up, and you're ready to begin organizing your first class.

2. Navigating the Google Classroom Dashboard

After creating your account and class, you'll be directed to your **Google Classroom dashboard**. Here, you'll see a streamlined, easy-to-navigate interface that organizes everything you need for managing your class.

Key Sections of the Dashboard:

1. **Stream:**

   - o This is your class's main feed. The Stream is where you post announcements, updates, and discussions. It works similarly to a social media feed, where students can comment and engage with the posts.

- You can create posts with important information, resources, and updates that will be visible to all of your students.

2. **Classwork**:

   - This tab is where you'll organize and post assignments, materials, and projects for your students. You can categorize assignments by topics (e.g., Week 1, Chapter 2, etc.) to keep things organized.

   - You can also track due dates, post quizzes, and share class resources from this section.

3. **People**:

   - In this tab, you can see all the participants in your class. As a teacher, you'll have access to your students' contact information and their roles within the classroom. You can also invite students or co-teachers and manage their permissions.

4. **Grades**:

   - The **Grades** section shows all of your students' assignments, grades, and feedback. You can see students' individual progress on assignments and provide grades and comments directly in this section.

5. **Settings (Gear Icon)**:

   - The gear icon in the top-right corner takes you to **Class Settings**, where you can adjust the overall setup for your class, including:

     - Changing the class name or description.

     - Managing permissions for who can post and comment in the Stream.

- Setting grading preferences and enabling/disabling specific features (like Google Meet integration).

- Creating a unique class code that students will use to join your class.

3. Setting Up Your First Class

Now that you've familiarized yourself with the Google Classroom interface, it's time to set up your first class. This step involves customizing your class, adding materials, and making sure your students know how to join.

How to Set Up Your First Class:

1. **Customize Your Class Theme:**

   o In the **Stream** tab, you can customize the look of your class by choosing a theme or uploading your own image. This adds a personal touch and can make your classroom feel more engaging for students.

   o Click on the **Select Theme** button in the class banner area to choose from pre-loaded themes or upload an image that represents your class.

2. **Create Your First Assignment:**

   o Navigate to the **Classwork** tab and click **Create** to begin adding content to your class. You can create:

      - **Assignments**: Create a task with detailed instructions, a due date, and options to add attachments (documents, links, videos, etc.).

      - **Quizzes**: Use Google Forms to create quizzes and share them with your students. This feature integrates smoothly with Classroom.

      - **Questions**: Post a question to start a class discussion or check students' understanding.

- **Materials**: Upload reading materials, slides, or resources that students will need.

When creating an assignment, you'll have the option to:

- o Attach a Google Doc, Slide, or Sheet for students to complete.

- o Set a due date and grading criteria.

- o Provide instructions or supplementary materials for students to refer to.

3. **Invite Students**:

- o In the **People** tab, you can manually invite students by email or share your class code with them. Students will use this code to join the class.

- o To find the class code, click the **Class Code** button in the **Class Settings** section. You can display it on your screen for students to enter directly, or share it through email or other communication methods.

4. **Post an Announcement**:

- o To keep students informed, post an announcement in the **Stream** tab. This can include important class details, reminders, or a welcome message. Students can also comment on announcements if you enable the option.

- o Click **Create** in the **Stream** tab and select **Announcement**. You can add text, attach files, and choose whether students can comment on the post.

4. Organizing and Customizing Your Classroom for Success

Once your class is set up, it's important to keep things organized and tailored to your teaching style and students' needs. Google Classroom offers several features to help you manage your class effectively.

Tips for Organizing Your Google Classroom:

1. **Use Topics to Categorize Assignments:**

   o In the **Classwork** tab, you can create **Topics** (e.g., Week 1, Chapter 1, Homework, etc.) to categorize your assignments. This helps students easily navigate and locate materials by topic or week.

   o Click on **Create** and select **Topic** to create different categories for your assignments and resources.

2. **Establish a Consistent Routine:**

   o Set a regular schedule for posting assignments and updates. Whether you post weekly assignments or have daily discussions, maintaining consistency will help students manage their workload and stay engaged.

   o Ensure that your students know where to find assignments, resources, and announcements by keeping the organization of the **Stream** and **Classwork** sections clean and up-to-date.

3. **Use the Google Meet Integration for Live Sessions:**

   o If you plan to host live video sessions with your class, Google Classroom integrates seamlessly with **Google Meet**. You can generate a Google Meet link for each class, which will appear in the **Classwork** or **Stream** tabs.

   o To create a Meet link, go to **Class Settings**, and enable the **Generate Google Meet link** option. You can share this link in announcements or as part of assignments.

4. **Communicate and Collaborate:**

   o Use the **Stream** for announcements and updates, but also encourage students to use it for asking questions, sharing resources, or engaging in discussions. You can foster a sense of community in your virtual classroom by allowing students to interact and collaborate.

- o Set rules for using the Stream, such as limiting comments to class-related discussions, to ensure it remains a productive space.

By following these steps, you'll have a fully set-up Google Classroom ready to engage your students and streamline your teaching process. In the next chapters, we'll dive deeper into how to create assignments, grade work, and use Google Classroom's powerful tools to enhance your teaching.

Chapter 2: Assignments and Grading

One of the main functions of Google Classroom is managing assignments and grading. This chapter will guide you through the process of creating and assigning assignments, organizing them for better tracking, and providing feedback to students. We will also discuss how to add resources to your assignments and set due dates to keep students on track. By the end of this chapter, you'll be well-equipped to handle the assignments and grading process effectively within Google Classroom.

1. Creating and Assigning Assignments to Students

Creating assignments in Google Classroom is a simple and efficient way to distribute tasks to students and track their progress. Assignments can be customized with specific instructions, due dates, and grading criteria, allowing you to tailor them to your curriculum.

Steps to Create an Assignment:

1. **Go to the Classwork Tab**:

   o Navigate to the **Classwork** tab in your Google Classroom. This is where all your assignments, materials, and quizzes will be located.

2. **Click on Create**:

   o In the **Classwork** tab, click the **Create** button. This will open a dropdown menu where you can select **Assignment** to create a new task for your students.

3. **Add Assignment Details**:

   o **Title**: Enter a clear and concise title for your assignment (e.g., "Essay on The Great Gatsby").

- o **Instructions**: Provide detailed instructions so students understand what's expected of them. You can also add additional guidelines, rubrics, or expectations here.

4. **Attach Materials**:

- o You can attach documents, presentations, videos, or links by clicking the **Add** button and selecting from Google Drive, links, files, or YouTube. This is especially useful for providing students with resources or reference materials.

5. **Assign to Specific Students (Optional)**:

- o If you want to assign the task to specific students or groups, click the **All Students** dropdown and select the students who should receive the assignment.

6. **Click Assign**:

- o After filling in the necessary details, click **Assign** to distribute the assignment to your students. Alternatively, you can schedule it to be posted later or save it as a draft.

2. Organizing Assignments by Topics or Units

Organizing your assignments into topics or units is essential for keeping your Google Classroom streamlined and easy to navigate. This allows both you and your students to find assignments easily and keep track of progress.

How to Organize Assignments:

1. **Create Topics**:

- o In the **Classwork** tab, you can create **Topics** to categorize assignments by theme, unit, week, or any system that makes sense for your course.

- o To create a topic, click the **Create** button in the Classwork tab and select **Topic**. You can name the topic something like "Week 1: Introduction to Geometry" or "Unit 3: World War II."

2. **Assign Assignments to Topics**:

   o When creating an assignment, quiz, or material, you can select which topic the assignment belongs to. Simply choose the relevant topic from the **Topic** dropdown menu when you are setting up the assignment.

   o You can always change or add a topic to an existing assignment by editing the assignment and selecting the appropriate topic.

3. **Reorganize Topics**:

   o If needed, you can easily rearrange topics by dragging them up or down in the Classwork tab. This makes it easy to adjust the flow of your assignments or lessons.

Why Organizing by Topics is Important:

- **Improved Navigation**: Students can easily find their assignments by topic or unit, allowing them to focus on the material they need.

- **Clearer Class Structure**: A well-organized classroom makes it easier to track progress and ensure students are completing tasks in the correct order.

- **Time-Saving**: Both you and your students can quickly locate specific assignments without wasting time searching.

3. Adding Attachments and Resources to Assignments

Google Classroom makes it easy to attach documents, videos, and other resources directly to assignments. This is useful when you need to provide students with reference materials, instructions, or additional learning resources.

Steps to Add Attachments:

1. **While Creating an Assignment**:

- When creating or editing an assignment, click the **Add** button (which looks like a paperclip icon).
- You can choose to add files from Google Drive, upload files from your computer, share a link, or even add a YouTube video.

2. **Using Google Drive**:
   - If you want to add a file from your Google Drive, click the **Google Drive** option and browse for the document, spreadsheet, presentation, or folder you wish to add.
   - You can also create new Google Docs, Sheets, or Slides by clicking **Create** and choosing the appropriate option.

3. **Adding a YouTube Video**:
   - If you want to embed a YouTube video into the assignment, click **Add** and select **YouTube**. You can search for the video directly in the search bar or paste a YouTube URL if you already have the link.

4. **Adding Links**:
   - You can also add external links, such as web pages, articles, or resources from other platforms. Just click **Add** and select **Link**, then paste the URL.

5. **Sharing with Students**:
   - After adding all necessary attachments, students will be able to access these resources when they open the assignment. They can view, edit (if given permission), or download the attached materials as needed.

4. Setting Due Dates and Deadlines

Due dates and deadlines help ensure that students stay on track and complete their assignments on time. Google Classroom allows you to easily set due dates for each assignment and helps you track student progress.

How to Set Due Dates:

1. **Set a Due Date When Creating an Assignment**:

   o While creating or editing an assignment, scroll down to the **Due Date** section.

   o Click the **Due Date** dropdown and select the specific date and time when the assignment is due.

   o You can set the time by selecting the **Time** box, which will default to the time you are creating the assignment, but you can adjust it based on your needs.

2. **Adjust or Remove Due Dates**:

   o You can always adjust or remove the due date after the assignment has been posted. Simply edit the assignment and update the **Due Date** field.

Why Due Dates are Important:

- **Encourages Timely Completion**: Setting due dates creates a sense of urgency and helps students prioritize their tasks.

- **Better Tracking**: Teachers can use due dates to track which students have completed assignments on time and which students need reminders or extensions.

- **Clarifies Expectations**: Students will clearly know when their assignments are due, reducing confusion and promoting accountability.

5. Grading and Providing Feedback on Assignments

Grading and providing feedback in Google Classroom is straightforward. It allows you to quickly grade assignments, provide comments, and return them to students. This feature helps keep students engaged and provides them with the necessary guidance to improve.

How to Grade Assignments:

1. **Open the Assignment**:
    - o Once students have submitted their assignments, navigate to the **Grades** tab or the **Classwork** tab and click on the assignment you wish to grade.

2. **Grade Using the Gradebook**:
    - o In the **Grade** section, you can input numerical grades or use a rubric (if you've created one) to evaluate the assignment. Google Classroom allows you to assign points or use letter grades.

3. **Provide Feedback**:
    - o After grading, click on the **Private Comment** section to leave specific feedback for individual students. You can provide encouragement, notes on what they did well, and suggestions for improvement.
    - o You can also add comments on specific parts of the assignment, especially if students submitted a Google Doc, Slide, or Sheet. These comments appear directly on the student's work for easy reference.

4. **Return Graded Assignments**:
    - o After grading and providing feedback, click the **Return** button. This sends the graded assignment back to the student and allows them to review your comments.

Why Grading and Feedback are Important:

- **Encourages Improvement**: Providing clear, constructive feedback helps students understand where they can improve and what they did well.

- **Keeps Students Engaged**: Regular grading and feedback motivate students to stay on top of their work and ensure they are actively learning from their mistakes.

- **Saves Time**: Google Classroom streamlines the grading process by automatically organizing and tracking student submissions, so you spend less time managing papers and more time interacting with students.

With these tools in Google Classroom, you can easily manage assignments, provide feedback, and maintain a smooth workflow for grading and tracking student progress. In the next chapter, we'll explore how to enhance your virtual classroom experience by fostering communication and collaboration with students.

Chapter 3: Managing Student Enrollment

One of the essential aspects of running an effective online classroom is managing student enrollment and ensuring that students are engaged and actively participating. Google Classroom offers several tools to help you invite, organize, and monitor students as they progress through your course. This chapter will walk you through how to invite students to your classroom, organize them into groups, and track their participation and progress to ensure they are staying on top of their assignments and learning.

1. Inviting and Adding Students to Your Classroom

Inviting students to your Google Classroom is one of the first steps in setting up your online course. Google Classroom makes it easy to invite students via email, share a class code, or add them manually if necessary.

Steps to Invite Students:

1. **Access the People Tab:**

     o   Go to your **Google Classroom dashboard** and select the class you want to add students to. Click on the **People** tab at the top of the page.

2. **Invite Students via Email:**

     o   In the **People** tab, click the **Invite Students** button.

     o   You'll be prompted to enter the email addresses of your students. You can manually type them in or paste a list of emails.

     o   After entering the emails, click **Invite**. Students will receive an invitation to join the class via email, and they can accept the invitation by clicking on the link provided.

3. **Use the Class Code**:

   o   Alternatively, you can share your **class code** with students to allow them to join your class.

   o   The **class code** can be found in the **Class Settings** (click the gear icon in the top-right corner of your Classroom page). You'll see a unique code for your class.

   o   Share the class code with students through email, messaging platforms, or even on a physical syllabus. Students will simply click **Join Class** in Google Classroom and enter the code to join.

4. **Add Students Manually**:

   o   If you need to manually add students, you can do so by entering their email addresses directly in the **Invite Students** section or by having them enter the class code.

5. **Manage Student Roles**:

   o   As the teacher, you automatically have the **Teacher** role. You can also assign co-teachers if you want other instructors to assist with managing the class. To add a co-teacher, click **Invite Teachers** in the **People** tab and enter their email addresses.

   o   Co-teachers will have similar permissions to the main teacher, such as posting assignments, grading, and managing students.

Why This is Important:

- **Easy Enrollment**: Google Classroom provides multiple options for inviting students, making it accessible for all types of learning environments (online, hybrid, in-person).

- **Flexibility**: The ability to share the class code gives you flexibility in how you distribute access to your class, especially if you're using Classroom in conjunction with other platforms or in a live classroom.

2. Organizing Students into Groups

For many teachers, having students work in groups can foster collaboration, enhance learning, and improve engagement. Google Classroom makes it easy to organize students into groups for projects, discussions, or peer review tasks.

How to Organize Students into Groups:

1. **Manual Grouping**:

   o In the **People** tab, you'll see a list of all your students. If you want to group students manually, you can use this list as a reference and assign students to groups.

   o For example, you might want to assign **Group 1**, **Group 2**, and so on, based on the class list. You can label the groups within the **Classwork** tab or in your assignment instructions.

2. **Using Google Classroom's Grouping Feature for Assignments**:

   o When creating an assignment, you can assign it to specific groups of students by choosing the "**All students**" dropdown menu and selecting only the students in that group. This allows you to assign the same task to a group of students, while others are working on different assignments.

3. **Google Meet Integration for Group Collaboration**:

   o If you plan to have students meet virtually, you can schedule separate **Google Meet sessions** for each group directly from within Google Classroom.

   o After organizing your groups, you can share a **Google Meet link** in each group's assignment, enabling them to have private discussions or work on collaborative projects.

4. **Using Google Docs, Sheets, or Slides for Group Collaboration**:

   o If you want students to work on a group assignment using Google Docs, Sheets, or Slides, you can create a shared document or presentation and assign it to specific groups.

   o Google Classroom allows you to automatically share documents with students, and each group can collaborate on the same file in real time.

5. **Monitor Group Progress**:

   o You can track how each group is progressing by reviewing the work they submit or through Google Docs' version history feature, which shows real-time changes and contributions.

Why Grouping is Important:

- **Fosters Collaboration**: Organizing students into groups enhances collaboration, which is essential for active learning.

- **Promotes Engagement**: Group work encourages students to actively participate and learn from their peers, which can improve understanding and retention of course material.

- **Easier Management**: Google Classroom's grouping feature allows you to assign tasks, monitor group progress, and provide feedback to each group individually, making the process more manageable.

3. Managing Student Progress and Tracking Participation

As a teacher, keeping track of student progress and participation is essential to understanding how well students are engaging with the material and meeting course objectives. Google Classroom makes it simple to monitor each student's work and provide feedback as needed.

How to Track Student Progress:

1. **View Individual Student Submissions:**

   o In the **Classwork** tab, click on any assignment to view how each student has submitted their work. You can see whether they've turned it in, if it's late, and any comments they've left.

   o You can also access individual student submissions directly from the **Gradebook** in the **Grades** tab, where you can see their grades for all assignments, their progress over time, and overall performance.

2. **Use the To-Do List:**

   o The **To-Do List** in Google Classroom helps both you and your students stay on top of assignments. It shows upcoming assignments and due dates. Students will see which assignments are due and which they've completed, while you can easily track the status of all students' submissions.

   o As assignments are graded, the **To-Do List** updates to show whether an assignment has been completed and graded, providing both teachers and students a clear view of progress.

3. **Gradebook Overview:**

   o The **Gradebook** tab offers an overview of each student's performance on all assignments. You can see their grades, provide private feedback, and track overall performance in your class.

   o You can also export the gradebook to a **Google Sheet** for further analysis or to import grades into your school's grading system.

4. **Monitor Class Participation**:

   o Google Classroom tracks how much time students spend on their assignments and when they complete them. While it doesn't give detailed engagement analytics (like how much time they spent reading materials), it provides a broad picture of when students are participating and submitting their work.

   o Use the **Stream** to track student interaction with announcements and discussions. You can see who is commenting, asking questions, or posting responses.

5. **Communication and Check-Ins**:

   o Regular communication is key to tracking student progress. You can use the **Stream** to send quick reminders or check-ins to the class. Encourage students to ask questions or post comments about any challenges they're facing.

   o For one-on-one check-ins, you can send **private comments** on assignments or use the **People** tab to send direct messages to students.

Why Monitoring Student Progress is Important:

- **Early Intervention**: Tracking progress allows you to spot students who might be struggling and offer help before they fall behind.

- **Increased Accountability**: Keeping students accountable for their assignments and participation fosters responsibility and keeps them engaged in their learning.

- **Continuous Feedback**: Regular monitoring and feedback help students stay on track and understand where they need to improve.

With Google Classroom, managing student enrollment, organizing groups, and tracking progress is streamlined and efficient. These features allow you to keep your students organized, provide valuable feedback, and monitor their performance in real time. In the next chapter, we'll explore how to make the most of Google Classroom's communication features to engage your students and foster a collaborative online environment.

Chapter 4: Communication with Students

Effective communication is essential in any classroom, and this is especially true in an online environment. Google Classroom offers several tools to help you keep students informed, engaged, and connected. Whether you're posting announcements, sending private messages, facilitating class discussions, or encouraging student interactions, Google Classroom provides a range of communication features that streamline the process. In this chapter, we'll walk you through the best ways to communicate with your students using Google Classroom's built-in tools.

1. Posting Announcements and Updates

Posting announcements is one of the easiest and most effective ways to communicate important information to your class. Announcements can be used to share updates, reminders, instructions, or any other key information that all students need to know.

How to Post Announcements:

1. **Go to the Stream Tab**:

   o The **Stream** is where all your class communications happen. To post an announcement, go to the **Stream** tab in your Google Classroom.

2. **Click on Create**:

   o In the Stream, click the **Create** button and select **Announcement** from the dropdown menu.

3. **Write Your Announcement**:

   o **Title**: You can provide a title, although this is optional. It's a good idea to make your announcement's title clear and to the point (e.g., "Reminder: Assignment Due Friday").

- Message: Enter your message in the **Message** box. Here you can provide detailed information or instructions that students need to know. You can include resources, such as links, attachments, or videos, to support the announcement.

4. **Add Attachments (Optional):**

- If you want to include additional materials (such as documents, links, or videos), click the **Add** button below the message box to upload files from Google Drive, attach links, or add YouTube videos.

5. **Post to Specific Students (Optional):**

- If the announcement is only relevant to certain students or groups, you can select **Specific Students** from the **All Students** dropdown menu.

6. **Click Post:**

- Once you're happy with your announcement, click **Post** to send it out to the class. All students will receive a notification on their end, letting them know they have a new update.

Why Announcements are Important:

- **Streamlined Communication**: Announcements serve as a central place for important class updates, making it easy for students to keep up-to-date with changes or new information.

- **Visibility**: Announcements are prominently displayed in the Stream and are easily accessible, ensuring that all students receive the message.

- **Engagement**: Well-timed announcements help maintain students' attention and remind them of upcoming deadlines, events, or required actions.

2. Sending Private Messages to Students

Sometimes, you'll need to communicate directly with individual students to provide feedback, address concerns, or answer questions. Google Classroom allows you to send private messages to students, ensuring that communication remains confidential.

How to Send Private Messages:

1. **Navigate to the People Tab**:

    o   Click on the **People** tab at the top of your Google Classroom. This will display a list of all students in your class.

2. **Select the Student**:

    o   Find the student you want to contact and click on their name. This will open a direct view of their information, including their submitted assignments and participation in the class.

3. **Send a Private Comment**:

    o   Below the student's name, you'll see an option to **Private Comment**. This allows you to send a direct message to the student that only they can see.

    o   Enter your message, and click **Send**.

Why Private Messages are Important:

*   **Personalized Communication**: Private messages allow you to give individual attention to students who need extra help, have questions, or need guidance without distracting other students.

*   **Confidentiality**: Direct communication ensures that sensitive information or feedback is kept confidential.

*   **Direct Support**: These messages help build stronger relationships between you and your students and encourage open, honest communication.

3. Using the Stream Feature for Class Discussions

The **Stream** isn't just for announcements; it's also an excellent place for class discussions, allowing students to interact with each other and with you. The Stream feature encourages real-time interaction, which is essential for maintaining a dynamic and engaging virtual classroom.

How to Use the Stream for Class Discussions:

1. **Create a Discussion Prompt**:
   - In the **Stream** tab, click the **Create** button and select **Question** from the dropdown menu.

2. **Write Your Discussion Question**:
   - **Question Title**: Enter a question or prompt that encourages student responses. Make sure the question is open-ended to promote thoughtful discussion (e.g., "What are the key themes in Chapter 5 of 'The Great Gatsby'?").
   - **Options for Responses**: Choose whether you want students to answer publicly or privately. You can also allow students to comment on each other's answers.

3. **Add Attachments or Resources** (Optional):
   - You can add documents, videos, links, or any other resources that may help students respond to the discussion prompt. For example, you could link to an article or video that provides context for the discussion.

4. **Post the Question**:
   - Once you've set up the question, click **Ask**. The question will appear in the Stream, and students will be able to respond in the comment section.

5. **Engage with Students**:
   - Encourage students to reply to each other's answers, share insights, and ask follow-up questions. This will

foster a deeper discussion and create an interactive learning environment.

Why Class Discussions are Important:

- **Encourages Engagement**: Discussions foster a sense of community and encourage students to engage with the material and their peers.

- **Promotes Critical Thinking**: Open-ended questions prompt students to think critically and express their ideas in a collaborative environment.

- **Real-Time Interaction**: The Stream feature allows you to respond to students in real time, creating a dynamic, ongoing conversation that mimics a physical classroom's interaction.

4. Encouraging Interaction through Comments

Comments are an essential tool for fostering interaction between you and your students, as well as among the students themselves. Google Classroom allows you to provide comments on assignments, announcements, and class discussions, promoting communication and feedback.

How to Use Comments Effectively:

1. **Comment on Assignments**:

   o After students submit assignments, you can provide feedback directly on the assignment itself. Simply open the assignment, scroll down to the student's submission, and click **Add a Comment**.

   o You can leave both general feedback and specific comments on the student's work. Google Classroom also allows you to leave **private comments** for students, visible only to them.

2. **Comment in Class Discussions**:

- When a student answers a question in the Stream, you can reply to their comment to ask further questions, provide feedback, or engage with the discussion.

- Encourage students to comment on each other's responses, as this promotes collaboration and peer-to-peer learning.

3. **Encourage Student Comments**:

- Ask students to comment on each other's posts or assignments. This helps foster a collaborative learning environment where students can learn from each other's perspectives.

- Use comments to ask guiding questions that challenge students to think more deeply about the material or to clarify any points of confusion.

Why Comments are Important:

- **Constructive Feedback**: Comments provide a space for you to offer valuable, constructive feedback to students on their work, helping them improve.

- **Encouraging Peer Learning**: Encouraging students to comment on each other's work or responses creates a collaborative and interactive learning environment.

- **Clarification**: Students can use comments to ask follow-up questions or seek clarification on course material or assignments, ensuring they remain on track.

Conclusion

Google Classroom provides several powerful tools for communicating with students, fostering engagement, and creating a supportive virtual classroom. Whether you are posting announcements, engaging in class discussions, sending private messages, or encouraging student interaction through comments, these features help you stay connected with your students and facilitate a positive, collaborative learning environment. By mastering these communication tools, you can create a more dynamic and interactive experience for your students, ensuring they stay informed, engaged, and motivated throughout the course. In the next chapter, we'll explore how to manage and track student assignments and progress effectively using Google Classroom's grading tools.

Chapter 5: Google Classroom Tools and Integrations

Google Classroom is an incredibly versatile platform, offering a wide range of tools and integrations that can enhance the learning experience for both you and your students. By integrating popular Google tools like Google Docs, Sheets, and Slides, as well as external third-party apps, you can create a dynamic and interactive classroom that supports collaboration, real-time communication, and efficient content creation. In this chapter, we will explore how to use these tools and integrations to streamline your teaching, improve student collaboration, and enrich the overall learning process.

1. Integrating Google Docs, Google Sheets, and Google Slides

Google Classroom seamlessly integrates with key Google Workspace tools like Google Docs, Sheets, and Slides, making it easier for you to create, share, and collaborate on assignments and resources.

How to Integrate Google Docs, Sheets, and Slides:

1. **Create Google Docs, Sheets, or Slides for Assignments**:

   o When creating an assignment, quiz, or material in the **Classwork** tab, click **Create** and select **Google Docs**, **Google Sheets**, or **Google Slides**. This will open a blank document, sheet, or slide deck that you can customize and share directly with your students.

   o After creating the file, it is automatically saved in your Google Drive and attached to the assignment in Google Classroom.

2. **Assign to Students**:

   o Once the file is created, you can assign it to your students. Google Classroom allows you to share these files with students in a "view," "comment," or "edit" mode. For collaborative work, you might choose **edit** mode, allowing students to work on the same document simultaneously.

o To assign the document, simply add it to the assignment, and choose whether you want each student to get their own copy of the document, or if you're sharing a single copy that everyone will edit.

3. **Student Collaboration**:

o When students open the file, they can edit it, leave comments, and collaborate in real time. You can track their progress by reviewing the document's version history, which shows who made changes and when. This feature is especially useful for group projects.

4. **Feedback and Grading**:

o Once students submit their work, you can review the document directly within Google Classroom. You can add comments or highlight text within the document itself. You can also leave overall feedback and grade assignments directly through Google Classroom.

Why Google Docs, Sheets, and Slides are Essential:

- **Collaboration**: These tools allow students to work together in real-time, enhancing collaboration on projects and assignments.

- **Efficient Feedback**: You can leave inline comments and track changes in shared documents, making it easier to provide specific, detailed feedback.

- **Seamless Integration**: The integration with Google Classroom makes the entire process of creating, sharing, submitting, and grading documents seamless.

2. Using Google Meet for Video Conferences

Google Meet is integrated with Google Classroom, providing an easy way to conduct virtual classes, office hours, or group discussions. Google Meet allows you to interact with your students in real-time, delivering lectures, hosting Q&A sessions, and facilitating discussions.

How to Use Google Meet in Google Classroom:

1. **Schedule a Google Meet Session**:

   ○ When creating an assignment or announcement in the **Classwork** or **Stream** tabs, you can add a **Google Meet** link. Click **Add Google Meet Link** when creating the post.

   ○ The generated Meet link will appear in the announcement or assignment, and students can click it to join the meeting at the scheduled time.

2. **Conducting Live Classes**:

   ○ You can use Google Meet to hold live video lessons. To start the meeting, simply click the link you created in Google Classroom. You can share your screen, present slides, or record the session for students who are unable to attend live.

   ○ During the meeting, you can use features such as **breakout rooms** for small group discussions, screen sharing for presentations, and **mute/unmute** controls to manage the class.

3. **Scheduling Office Hours or Review Sessions**:

   ○ Google Meet is also perfect for scheduling one-on-one office hours or small group review sessions. You can create a recurring meeting link for your office hours and share it with students in advance.

4. **Security Features**:

- Google Meet provides security features like **muting participants, controlling who can enter the meeting,** and the ability to **remove disruptive participants**. These features help you maintain a professional and secure virtual classroom environment.

Why Google Meet is Important for Virtual Classes:

- **Real-Time Interaction**: Google Meet allows for direct, live communication with students, enhancing the feeling of a traditional classroom environment.

- **Integrated with Google Classroom**: The ability to add a Meet link directly to Google Classroom streamlines the process of scheduling and joining virtual meetings.

- **Convenience**: Google Meet is easy to use, and its integration with Google Classroom means you can launch meetings with just a few clicks.

3. Adding Third-Party Educational Apps to Your Classroom

Google Classroom allows you to extend its functionality by integrating third-party educational apps. These apps can enhance the learning experience by offering additional resources, tools, and interactivity. Many of these apps are free or offer special pricing for educators.

How to Add Third-Party Apps:

1. **Explore the Google Classroom App Marketplace**:
   - To browse available third-party apps, go to **Google Classroom Settings**, and click on **Apps**.
   - In the **Google Workspace Marketplace**, you'll find a variety of educational apps designed to work with Google Classroom. These apps can help with everything from creating interactive quizzes and assignments to facilitating discussions or enhancing student collaboration.

2. **Add the App to Your Classroom**:

   ○ To add an app, click on the **Install** button next to the app you want to use, then follow the prompts to authorize the integration with your Google Classroom. Once added, the app will be available in your Google Classroom for all future assignments and tasks.

3. **Examples of Popular Third-Party Apps**:

   ○ **Kahoot!**: Create interactive quizzes and games to make learning fun and engaging.

   ○ **Edpuzzle**: Turn your videos into interactive lessons by adding questions, quizzes, and notes.

   ○ **Flipgrid**: Enable students to record and share videos on specific topics, fostering deeper engagement and peer learning.

   ○ **Pear Deck**: Create interactive presentations that allow students to participate directly by answering questions, drawing on slides, and more.

Why Third-Party Apps are Valuable:

- **Enhanced Learning**: Many third-party apps offer specialized tools that enhance the educational experience, such as interactive games, quizzes, and collaborative learning platforms.

- **Variety and Flexibility**: Adding apps allows you to diversify your teaching methods, providing students with different ways to engage with the material.

- **Seamless Integration**: Third-party apps integrate directly with Google Classroom, so you don't have to leave the platform to access additional tools or resources.

4. Using Google Drive for Collaborative Work

Google Drive is the backbone of Google Classroom, providing a cloud-based storage solution for all your class materials, assignments, and student work. It also offers powerful collaborative features, allowing you and your students to work together on documents, spreadsheets, presentations, and other materials.

How to Use Google Drive for Collaboration:

1. **Share Files with Students**:

   o When creating an assignment, you can easily attach a document from your **Google Drive**. You can choose whether students will have **view**, **comment**, or **edit** access to the document.

   o If you want to allow students to collaborate, select the **edit** access option so they can work together on a shared file in real-time.

2. **Create Collaborative Folders**:

   o You can create shared folders in Google Drive to organize class materials, assignments, or projects. These folders can be shared with students, allowing them to access the materials they need for class and collaborate on group assignments.

3. **Track Changes in Shared Documents**:

   o Google Drive's version history allows you to see who made changes to a document, when, and what changes were made. This feature is especially useful for group projects, as you can see how each student has contributed.

4. **Real-Time Editing**:

   o With tools like **Google Docs**, **Google Sheets**, and **Google Slides**, students can collaborate on assignments in real-time, making it easy for them to work together on projects and submit group work. You can track their progress and provide immediate feedback.

Why Google Drive is Essential for Collaboration:

- **Instant Collaboration**: Google Drive's real-time editing features enable students to work together on documents, making it easy to collaborate without version control issues or emailing files back and forth.

- **Organization**: Google Drive allows you to organize your class materials, assignments, and student submissions in a structured way that's easily accessible.

- **Efficiency**: Using Google Drive streamlines collaboration, allowing you to manage, edit, and provide feedback on student work in one centralized location.

Conclusion

Google Classroom's integration with Google Docs, Sheets, Slides, Google Meet, third-party educational apps, and Google Drive provides an all-in-one solution for organizing and enhancing your classroom. By leveraging these tools, you can foster a collaborative and interactive learning environment, encourage student engagement, and make your teaching more efficient and effective. In the next chapter, we'll dive deeper into how to track and manage student progress using Google Classroom's grading and analytics tools.

Chapter 6: Best Practices for Online Teaching with Google Classroom

As you grow more comfortable with Google Classroom, it's essential to implement best practices that will enhance your online teaching experience. Google Classroom offers a robust platform for managing assignments, providing feedback, and fostering communication, but using it effectively requires thoughtful organization, engaging lessons, and strategies for student collaboration. In this chapter, we'll explore best practices for organizing your Google Classroom, creating engaging lessons, using the Calendar feature to stay organized, and encouraging student collaboration and peer review.

1. Organizing Your Google Classroom for Maximum Efficiency

An organized Google Classroom helps you and your students navigate the platform easily, reduces confusion, and ensures that everything is in its proper place. A well-organized environment promotes efficiency, allowing you to focus on teaching and ensuring your students have a smooth learning experience.

How to Organize Google Classroom Efficiently:

1. **Create Clear Topics:**

    o Use the **Topics** feature in the **Classwork** tab to categorize assignments, materials, and resources. Organizing assignments by topics like "Week 1," "Unit 1: Introduction to Algebra," or "Chapter 3: Photosynthesis" makes it easier for students to find what they need.

    o Consistently apply topics across all assignments to create a uniform structure throughout the course. You can also add sub-topics to further categorize materials.

2. **Use the Classwork Tab Effectively**:

   o When creating assignments, quizzes, or materials, ensure they are attached to the appropriate topic for easy access. For example, if you are posting homework for Week 2, it should be categorized under "Week 2" as a topic.

   o Consider creating **"Weekly Reminders"** as a topic where you post a weekly schedule, important updates, or any special instructions.

3. **Limit Stream Posts**:

   o The **Stream** tab can quickly become cluttered with notifications and messages. To keep it clean, use the **Stream** primarily for important announcements, class updates, or time-sensitive information. All assignments and ongoing discussions should be posted in the **Classwork** tab.

4. **Use Folders for File Organization**:

   o Google Drive allows you to create folders for different types of documents (e.g., assignments, resources, class materials). Use shared Google Drive folders for each of your classes so you can easily access files without having to search through multiple folders.

Why Organization Matters:

- **Clarity and Ease of Use**: A well-organized Classroom makes it easier for students to find their assignments, course materials, and resources, reducing confusion.

- **Time Management**: Streamlining and organizing your teaching materials saves you time when posting, grading, and managing student work.

- **Consistent Structure**: Consistency in how you organize your content gives students a predictable environment, helping them stay focused and engaged.

2. Creating Engaging Lessons and Activities

Engaging students in an online setting requires creative and interactive lesson plans. Google Classroom allows you to incorporate multimedia, activities, and interactive assignments that can keep your students excited about the subject matter.

How to Create Engaging Lessons:

1. **Incorporate Multimedia**:
   - Use videos, images, and audio clips to enhance your lessons. For instance, you can attach a YouTube video, a recorded lecture, or an educational podcast to your assignments to provide different learning perspectives.
   - Encourage students to watch videos or listen to audio resources before or after class to reinforce lessons and keep them engaged in the material.

2. **Interactive Assignments**:
   - Use Google Docs, Sheets, and Slides to create interactive assignments. For example, you can set up collaborative Google Docs for group writing activities or have students create a **Google Slides** presentation for a project or research report.
   - Include **discussion questions** and **polls** in your assignments to promote interaction, critical thinking, and engagement.

3. **Gamify Learning**:
   - Integrate apps like **Kahoot!** or **Quizizz** into your Google Classroom for fun, interactive quizzes that turn learning into a game. These platforms allow you to create timed

quizzes, leaderboards, and challenges that motivate students to engage with the content.

4. **Incorporate Real-World Projects**:

   o Use project-based learning by assigning students tasks that require them to explore real-world applications of the subject matter. This could be a research project, a design challenge, or a case study analysis.

Why Engaging Lessons are Important:

- **Active Participation**: Engaging lessons and activities encourage students to actively participate, which helps them retain and apply what they're learning.

- **Increased Motivation**: Interactive and creative activities spark students' interest and make learning more enjoyable, which helps them stay motivated.

- **Diverse Learning Styles**: By incorporating various types of media and assignments, you can cater to different learning styles and preferences.

3. Using the Calendar Feature to Stay Organized

Google Classroom integrates with Google Calendar, which is a powerful tool for keeping both you and your students organized throughout the semester. By leveraging this feature, you can manage due dates, reminders, and live class sessions in one place.

How to Use Google Calendar in Google Classroom:

1. **Automatic Assignment Calendar Integration**:

   o When you create assignments in Google Classroom and set due dates, they are automatically added to your **Google Calendar**. This allows you and your students to see all upcoming deadlines in one view.

2. **Scheduling Live Classes with Google Meet**:

o   You can schedule live classes using Google Meet and sync them with Google Calendar. When creating an assignment or announcement, include the **Google Meet link** so students can easily access the meeting. The meeting will also appear in their Google Calendar with the scheduled time and link.

3. **Track Upcoming Deadlines**:

o   Google Calendar helps you keep track of important deadlines. You can set reminders for yourself and students to make sure that assignments, tests, and meetings are not missed.

4. **Customizing Events**:

o   You can add non-class-related events or activities to your Google Calendar, such as study sessions, office hours, or group work meetings. These events will appear alongside your assignments and class meetings, providing a complete schedule for your students.

Why Google Calendar is Useful:

- **Centralized Scheduling**: Calendar integration streamlines your schedule, ensuring that you never miss a deadline or class session.

- **Student Organization**: Students can view all their upcoming deadlines and events in their Google Calendar, helping them stay organized and on track.

- **Automatic Updates**: Google Classroom automatically syncs with Google Calendar, ensuring that both you and your students are always up-to-date.

4. Encouraging Student Collaboration and Peer Review

One of the main benefits of Google Classroom is its ability to promote collaboration among students, even in a remote setting. Encouraging students to work together, review each other's work, and provide feedback helps deepen their understanding and fosters a sense of community.

How to Foster Collaboration:

1. **Use Google Docs, Sheets, and Slides for Group Projects**:
   o Google Classroom makes it easy for students to collaborate on documents, spreadsheets, and presentations. When you create an assignment, you can select the option to share a document with **edit** access, allowing students to work together in real time.

   o Encourage students to use these tools for group projects or assignments that require collaborative input. Google Docs allows for easy commenting and suggestions, which can be reviewed by peers.

2. **Peer Review Assignments**:
   o Peer review is an effective way for students to learn from each other and improve their work. In Google Classroom, you can create assignments where students must submit their work, then review and provide constructive feedback on their peers' submissions.

   o Use the **Private Comments** feature to guide students through the peer review process, providing instructions and feedback on how to evaluate each other's work.

3. **Collaborative Discussions**:
   o Create discussion threads in the **Stream** or **Classwork** tab to encourage peer-to-peer interaction. You can set up discussion questions, group debates, or reflective prompts that require students to comment on and respond to each other's ideas.

4. **Breakout Rooms via Google Meet**:

o   If you're conducting live lessons, use **Google Meet's breakout rooms** feature to divide students into smaller groups. They can work on projects, discuss topics, or review assignments in a more intimate setting before sharing their insights with the class.

Why Collaboration and Peer Review are Important:

- **Enhances Learning**: Students can gain new perspectives and deepen their understanding through peer feedback and collaborative work.

- **Develops Critical Skills**: Working with others helps students develop critical communication, problem-solving, and teamwork skills—valuable for both academic and professional growth.

- **Encourages Active Participation**: Collaborative activities make learning more interactive and engaging, motivating students to actively contribute and take ownership of their learning process.

Conclusion

Incorporating these best practices into your online teaching approach will not only enhance your own productivity but will also create a more engaging and effective learning experience for your students. By organizing your Google Classroom, creating engaging and interactive lessons, utilizing the Calendar feature for better organization, and fostering collaboration through student work and peer reviews, you'll be able to create a thriving online classroom that keeps students motivated and connected. In the next chapter, we'll explore how to effectively monitor student progress and provide valuable feedback to help your students succeed.

Chapter 7: Assessing Student Progress

Assessing student progress is a key part of the teaching process. Google Classroom offers a variety of tools that allow you to assess your students' understanding of the material, provide clear feedback, and track their overall performance. This chapter will explore how to create quizzes and surveys, use rubrics for transparent grading, and analyze student performance through reports and insights. By leveraging these tools, you can ensure that your students are meeting learning goals and receive the support they need to succeed.

1. Creating Quizzes and Surveys in Google Classroom

Quizzes and surveys are great tools for assessing student knowledge, collecting feedback, and gauging their understanding of the material. Google Classroom integrates seamlessly with **Google Forms**, which you can use to create quizzes and surveys that are automatically graded.

How to Create a Quiz or Survey:

1. **Access the Classwork Tab**:

   o In Google Classroom, navigate to the **Classwork** tab where you will create your quiz or survey.

2. **Click Create and Select Quiz Assignment**:

   o Click the **Create** button and select **Quiz Assignment** from the dropdown menu. This option automatically creates a Google Form that is linked to your assignment.

3. **Set Up the Google Form**:

   o After selecting **Quiz Assignment**, a new Google Form will open. Here, you can create multiple-choice, short answer, or other types of questions. You can also add multimedia such as videos or images to make the quiz more engaging.

- o For **auto-grading**, set correct answers for multiple-choice or checkbox questions by selecting the **Answer Key** option. You can also assign point values to each question.

4. **Add Instructions and Attachments**:

- o Enter any instructions you'd like students to follow. This could include information about how many questions are on the quiz, time limits, or expectations for completing the quiz.

- o You can also attach relevant files, documents, or resources for students to reference while completing the quiz.

5. **Set Due Date and Points**:

- o Set a **due date** and assign points for the quiz. You can also use the **rubric** feature (explained later) to provide specific criteria for grading.

6. **Send and Collect Responses**:

- o After setting everything up, click **Assign**. Students will now have access to the quiz through Google Classroom. Once they submit the quiz, you will be able to view their responses and see scores if you have set up automatic grading.

Why Quizzes and Surveys Are Important:

- • **Quick Feedback**: Quizzes provide immediate insights into how well students understand the material, helping you identify areas where they need further support.

- • **Engagement**: Using interactive quizzes can keep students engaged and help reinforce learning by providing instant feedback on their performance.

- **Data Collection**: Surveys are a great tool for gathering feedback from students about their experience with the course or for assessing their perceptions of certain concepts.

2. Using Rubrics for Transparent Grading

Rubrics provide a clear and structured way to evaluate student assignments, ensuring that grading is consistent and transparent. Google Classroom allows you to create custom rubrics for assignments, making it easier for students to understand the grading criteria and for you to provide detailed feedback.

How to Create and Use Rubrics:

1. **Create an Assignment**:

   o In the **Classwork** tab, click on **Create** and select **Assignment**.

2. **Add Rubric**:

   o After entering your assignment details (title, instructions, due date), scroll down to the **Rubric** section and click **Create Rubric**.

3. **Define the Criteria**:

   o In the rubric creation window, define the criteria by which you will grade the assignment (e.g., accuracy, creativity, grammar, etc.). Each criterion should be specific and related to the goals of the assignment.

4. **Set Levels of Achievement**:

   o Define different levels of performance for each criterion (e.g., Excellent, Good, Needs Improvement). For each level, provide a description and assign a point range or score.

   o This will help ensure that students understand what is expected for each level of performance.

5. **Save and Apply Rubric**:

- Once the rubric is complete, click **Save** and it will be automatically attached to your assignment. You can use the rubric when grading to give clear, objective feedback on each student's performance.

6. **Provide Feedback Based on the Rubric**:

   - When grading, use the rubric to evaluate the student's submission. You can assign scores for each criterion and leave comments to explain your grading decisions. Google Classroom will automatically calculate the total score based on the rubric.

Why Rubrics are Important:

- **Clear Expectations**: Rubrics make it clear to students how they will be graded, which can reduce confusion and help them focus on the important aspects of the assignment.

- **Consistent Grading**: Rubrics provide a standardized method of grading, ensuring that all students are evaluated based on the same criteria.

- **Constructive Feedback**: Rubrics allow you to give detailed feedback on specific aspects of a student's work, helping them understand their strengths and areas for improvement.

3. Analyzing Student Performance with Reports and Insights

Google Classroom offers tools for analyzing student performance, allowing you to track how well individual students or the entire class is doing. These insights help you identify trends, such as areas where students are struggling, and adjust your teaching strategies accordingly.

How to Analyze Student Performance:

1. **Access the Grades Tab**:

   - The **Grades** tab in Google Classroom provides an overview of student performance across all

114

assignments. You can see each student's grades, the overall class performance, and any assignments that are missing or incomplete.

2. **Track Individual Student Progress**:

    o   In the **Grades** tab, click on a specific student's name to view their individual performance on each assignment. This gives you a detailed look at how the student is progressing and where they may need additional support.

    o   You can also add private comments on each assignment to give personalized feedback or provide encouragement.

3. **Review Class Performance as a Whole**:

    o   Google Classroom's **Gradebook** also provides a summary of the entire class's performance. You can identify patterns in the class as a whole, such as if many students are struggling with a particular assignment or concept.

    o   This data can help you decide whether to revisit certain topics or adjust your teaching methods.

4. **Download Reports**:

    o   Google Classroom allows you to export the **gradebook** to a **Google Sheet**. This is useful for further analysis or for sharing with administrators or parents.

    o   You can also export assignment responses from **Google Forms** used for quizzes, enabling you to analyze quiz results or create custom reports.

5. **Use Insights to Improve Teaching**:

    o   If you notice that many students are performing poorly on certain assignments or assessments, use this data to adjust your lessons or offer additional review materials.

o   Student insights also give you a better understanding of how students are engaging with the material, allowing you to provide targeted support where it's needed most.

Why Analyzing Performance is Important:

- **Early Identification of Struggles**: By analyzing student performance, you can identify students who may be falling behind and offer timely support to help them succeed.

- **Data-Driven Decisions**: Performance reports give you valuable insights into how effective your teaching methods are and allow you to make data-driven adjustments to your lessons.

- **Improved Student Outcomes**: Tracking performance helps ensure that students are meeting learning objectives, and provides you with the tools needed to help them improve where necessary.

Conclusion

Assessing student progress is an integral part of online teaching, and Google Classroom offers a wide range of tools to make this process easier and more effective. Whether you're creating quizzes and surveys to assess knowledge, using rubrics for clear and transparent grading, or analyzing student performance with reports and insights, these tools help you track progress and provide valuable feedback. By leveraging Google Classroom's assessment tools, you can ensure that your students receive the support and guidance they need to succeed in your course. In the next chapter, we'll explore how to maintain engagement and motivation in your virtual classroom, even during challenging times.

Chapter 8: Troubleshooting Google Classroom

While Google Classroom is a powerful and efficient platform for managing assignments and communication, like any software, it can sometimes present challenges. Being able to troubleshoot and resolve common issues quickly ensures that your virtual classroom runs smoothly, allowing you to stay focused on teaching. In this chapter, we will explore common issues with assignments and grades, problems with student enrollment and invitations, and how to handle technical issues with Google Meet and Google Docs.

1. Common Issues with Assignments and Grades

Assignments and grades are at the core of your online classroom experience, but they can occasionally present challenges. Whether students are having trouble submitting assignments or discrepancies appear in grading, it's essential to know how to resolve these issues efficiently.

Common Assignment Issues and Solutions:

1. **Students Can't Submit Assignments**:

   o **Issue**: Sometimes, students may not be able to submit their assignments, often due to the assignment being marked as "unsubmitted" or due to system glitches.

   o **Solution**:

     ▪ **Check Assignment Settings**: Ensure the assignment has been set up to accept submissions. You can do this by checking the assignment's **Due Date** and ensuring it's still open for submissions.

     ▪ **Reopen Assignment**: If a student missed the deadline, consider extending the deadline by editing the assignment and setting a new due date.

- **Ensure Students Are Using the Correct Link**: Sometimes, students may mistakenly use an old or incorrect link. Ensure they are accessing the correct assignment from Google Classroom.

2. **Missing or Incorrect Grades**:

   o **Issue**: Grades may not sync properly, or students may see incorrect grades.

   o **Solution**:

     - **Check for Manual Entry Errors**: Make sure that you haven't accidentally entered the wrong grades in the **Gradebook**. Double-check the grade and the point scale.

     - **Ensure Rubrics are Applied**: If you're using a rubric to grade, ensure that all criteria are filled in correctly and that the correct score is assigned to each criterion.

     - **Recalculate Grades**: Sometimes, recalculating grades may resolve discrepancies. You can manually refresh or adjust scores in the **Gradebook**

3. **Students Receiving the Wrong Feedback**:

   o **Issue**: Students may see the wrong feedback or comments on their assignments.

   o **Solution**:

     - **Review Private Comments**: Check that the feedback and comments you leave are directed to the correct student. Google Classroom allows you to add private comments, so make sure they are assigned properly.

- **Verify Comments Visibility**: Confirm that you are leaving feedback in the right section (e.g., assignment comments vs. class comments).

4. **Issues with File Attachments in Assignments**:

    o **Issue**: Sometimes, attachments don't appear or students can't open them.

    o **Solution**:

        - **File Permissions**: Make sure the files you attach to assignments have the correct sharing permissions. They should be set to **Anyone with the link** or **Viewable by students**.

        - **File Format**: Ensure that the files you're uploading are in formats that are accessible to all students. Common file formats like PDFs, Word Docs, and Google Docs should work without issues.

2. Solving Problems with Student Enrollment and Invitations

Issues related to student enrollment and invitations can prevent your students from joining your Google Classroom or accessing course materials. These problems are usually related to invitations, class codes, or permissions.

Common Enrollment Issues and Solutions:

1. **Students Cannot Join with the Class Code**:

    o **Issue**: Students may encounter difficulties when trying to join the class with the class code, such as receiving an error message that the code is invalid.

    o **Solution**:

        - **Check for Expired Class Code**: The class code may have expired or been deactivated. If this happens, generate a new class code from the **Class Settings** section and share it with your students.

- **Recheck the Code**: Ensure the code you provided to the students is typed correctly or copy the code directly from the Google Classroom platform.

- **Limitations on Join Attempts**: Ensure that the student is not already enrolled. If they are, Google Classroom will prevent them from joining again.

2. **Student Invitations Not Received**:

   o **Issue**: Students may report that they never received the invitation to join the class.

   o **Solution**:

      - **Verify Email Addresses**: Double-check that the email addresses you used for invitations are correct and active. If needed, re-invite the student by entering their correct email address.

      - **Spam Filters**: Ask students to check their spam or junk folder. Sometimes, Google Classroom invitations may be flagged by email filters.

      - **Manually Add Students**: If the invitation still isn't working, you can add students manually by going to the **People** tab and entering their email address.

3. **Issues with Co-Teachers or Admin Access**:

   o **Issue**: Co-teachers or teaching assistants may not have the correct permissions, preventing them from accessing or managing the class.

   o **Solution**:

- **Check Role Permissions**: In the **People** tab, verify that you've correctly assigned roles to your co-teachers and teaching assistants. Co-teachers should have the **Teacher** role, which allows them to create assignments and grade work.

- **Reinvite Co-Teachers**: If a co-teacher is having trouble accessing the classroom, try removing them and sending a new invitation.

4. **Class Code Not Visible to Students**:

   - **Issue**: Students may not see the class code, preventing them from joining the class on their own.

   - **Solution**:

     - **Display the Code**: Go to **Class Settings** and ensure that the class code is visible to students. You can display it publicly in the Stream or send it via email or a messaging platform.

     - **Alternative Invitations**: If the class code isn't working, try inviting students directly via email as an alternative method.

3. How to Handle Technical Issues with Google Meet and Google Docs

Sometimes technical issues arise with the tools integrated into Google Classroom, such as **Google Meet** for video conferencing or **Google Docs** for collaborative work. These issues may prevent you or your students from accessing meetings or editing shared documents, which can disrupt your teaching.

Google Meet Technical Issues:

1. **Students Can't Join Google Meet**:

- o **Issue**: Students may encounter issues when trying to join a Google Meet session, such as receiving an error message or being unable to connect.

- o **Solution:**

  - **Check Meet Link**: Ensure that you've provided the correct **Google Meet link** in Google Classroom. If you've set up the link for a recurring meeting, ensure that the link is still valid.

  - **Test the Link**: Before class, test the Meet link yourself to ensure it's working. If there's an issue with the link, generate a new one from the **Google Classroom** interface and post it again.

  - **Permissions**: If you've restricted access to the meeting (e.g., for invited members only), ensure that students have the correct permissions to join. In Google Meet settings, make sure that everyone has the ability to enter the meeting.

2. **Audio or Video Issues in Google Meet:**

   - o **Issue**: Participants may have problems with their audio or video during a Google Meet session, such as no sound or a frozen video feed.

   - o **Solution:**

     - **Check Microphone and Camera**: Ensure that students have their microphones and cameras properly configured and enabled. They should also check their device settings to ensure they are using the correct input/output devices (microphone and speakers).

     - **Bandwidth Issues**: If students experience lag or poor video quality, they should check their internet connection. Encourage them to turn off other high-bandwidth activities like streaming video or downloading large files.

- **Browser Compatibility**: Google Meet works best with Chrome. Ensure that students are using a compatible browser (preferably Chrome) and that it is updated to the latest version.

3. **Google Docs Not Loading or Syncing**:

   o **Issue**: Students may have trouble opening, editing, or saving documents in Google Docs, or documents may fail to sync.

   o **Solution**:

      - **Check Internet Connection**: Google Docs requires a stable internet connection to sync changes. If students are experiencing issues, they should check their connection and try refreshing the page.

      - **Clear Cache and Cookies**: Ask students to clear their browser cache and cookies if they are experiencing loading issues. This can often resolve syncing problems.

      - **Switch Browsers**: If the issue persists, students should try using a different browser or updating their current browser to ensure compatibility with Google Docs.

Why Troubleshooting Google Meet and Google Docs Is Important:

- **Maintaining Classroom Flow**: Quick resolution of technical issues ensures that class sessions run smoothly and students don't miss valuable learning time.

- **Clear Communication**: Ensuring that all students have access to video conferencing and collaborative tools like Google Docs helps maintain consistent communication and collaboration throughout the course.

Conclusion

Technical issues and challenges with Google Classroom can arise from time to time, but knowing how to troubleshoot common problems will help you quickly resolve them and keep your classroom running smoothly. Whether you're dealing with assignment submission issues, student enrollment problems, or technical difficulties with Google Meet or Google Docs, the solutions outlined in this chapter will ensure you're well-equipped to handle any situation. By addressing these issues efficiently, you'll maintain a positive and productive online learning environment for your students.

Conclusion

As we conclude this guide, it's important to take a moment to reflect on what you've learned and how you can continue to evolve as an online educator using Google Classroom. In this chapter, we will recap the key features of Google Classroom for beginners, explore how you can continue to grow in your online teaching journey, and outline the next steps for delving into advanced features to enhance your teaching even further.

1. Recap of Key Google Classroom Features for Beginners

Google Classroom is an incredibly versatile tool that streamlines teaching and helps you stay organized while connecting with your students in a virtual environment. Throughout this guide, we've covered the core features of Google Classroom that every beginner should know. Here's a quick recap:

- **Setting Up Google Classroom**: You learned how to create your Google Classroom, invite students, and organize your class for maximum efficiency. Whether through class codes or email invitations, getting your students into your virtual classroom is the first step.

- **Creating and Managing Assignments**: We explored how to create assignments, add materials, and use rubrics to grade student work transparently. Google Classroom also offers automatic grading for quizzes, saving you time while providing valuable feedback to your students.

- **Communication Tools**: Google Classroom's communication tools like announcements, private messages, and discussions on the Stream provide easy ways to interact with students, offer feedback, and keep them updated on class activities.

- **Integrating Google Tools**: Google Docs, Sheets, Slides, and Google Meet allow you to create engaging lessons and virtual meetings that integrate seamlessly with Google Classroom.

These tools help facilitate collaboration, enable real-time discussions, and provide students with multiple ways to interact with content.

- **Grading and Reporting**: You learned how to use Google Classroom's Gradebook to track and manage student progress, and how to use reports and insights to analyze student performance. The ability to quickly assess student work and provide feedback is crucial in maintaining an effective learning environment.

- **Troubleshooting and Problem-Solving**: You are now familiar with how to troubleshoot common issues with assignments, grades, and student invitations, ensuring that your Google Classroom experience remains smooth and productive.

2. Continuing Your Growth as an Online Educator

Becoming proficient with Google Classroom is just the beginning of your journey as an online educator. To continue growing and improving your skills, consider the following steps:

- **Stay Informed**: Google Classroom is constantly evolving with new features and updates. To stay up to date, regularly check the Google Classroom blog, participate in online educator communities, and attend webinars or training sessions. This will ensure you're aware of any new tools or best practices that can help enhance your teaching.

- **Experiment and Customize**: As you become more comfortable using Google Classroom, experiment with different teaching styles, assignment formats, and communication strategies. Google Classroom is flexible, so take advantage of that to create a learning environment that works best for you and your students.

- **Engage with the Community**: Join online forums, social media groups, or communities of Google Classroom users to share ideas, resources, and strategies. Connecting with other educators allows you to learn from others' experiences and get advice on how to improve your teaching practices.

- **Get Feedback from Your Students**: Regularly ask your students for feedback on the virtual learning experience. Understanding what works and what doesn't will help you refine your teaching methods, foster greater engagement, and support students in their learning.

3. Future Steps: Advanced Google Classroom Features to Explore

Once you're comfortable with the basics, Google Classroom offers a range of advanced features that can help you take your online teaching to the next level. Here are a few key areas to explore:

- **Google Classroom Extensions**:
  - Google Classroom integrates with a wide range of third-party apps and extensions, such as **Flipgrid, Edpuzzle, Kahoot!,** and more. These tools can help you gamify lessons, make content more interactive, and enhance student collaboration.

- **Differentiated Learning**:
  - You can customize assignments for individual students or groups, allowing you to tailor learning experiences to the unique needs of your students. For example, you can assign different tasks or materials to different groups or provide additional support for students who need it.

- **Using Google Classroom with Google Meet**:
  - Google Meet's integration with Google Classroom allows you to host live virtual classes, set up recurring meetings, and manage student participation. You can even record sessions for students who are unable to attend live meetings, making it easier to create a flexible learning environment.

- **Advanced Reporting and Analytics:**

  - Explore Google Classroom's reporting and insights features to gain a deeper understanding of student engagement, participation, and performance. Use these tools to identify trends, monitor class progress, and make data-driven decisions about your teaching strategies.

- **Google Classroom API for Customization:**

  - If you're comfortable with coding, Google Classroom offers an **API** (Application Programming Interface) that allows for more advanced customization and integration with other learning platforms or systems. This is ideal if you want to create a more personalized learning experience or integrate Classroom with your institution's LMS.

- **Creating and Managing Multiple Classrooms:**

  - If you're teaching multiple classes, explore how to manage and organize multiple Google Classrooms. Google Classroom offers features like **class grouping** and **batch processing**, making it easier to manage large amounts of student data across different courses.

Final Thoughts

Google Classroom offers a powerful set of tools for managing and enhancing your online teaching. By mastering the features covered in this guide, you can create an engaging, organized, and efficient virtual classroom that supports student learning. The journey to becoming an effective online educator doesn't stop here—there's always more to learn and explore. By staying informed, experimenting with new strategies, and embracing advanced features, you'll continue to improve as a digital educator and create an even better learning experience for your students.

As you move forward, take time to refine your practices, try new approaches, and keep pushing the boundaries of what's possible with Google Classroom. Your growth as an educator is a continuous process, and with the tools and strategies at your disposal, you are well on your way to creating a thriving online classroom.

www.ingramcontent.com/pod-product-compliance
Lightning Source LLC
Chambersburg PA
CBHW072200090426
42740CB00012B/2323